IMPROVE YOUR PLAY
AT TRUMP CONTRACTS

This book is aimed at improving your success rate when you are playing a trump contract. In contains eighty problems from actual play where the declarers involved either missed the winning line or found an excellent play, missed by other declarers. By trying to solve the problems yourself, you will gain experience in situations which you might not have previously encountered.

At no-trumps there is often merely one line for success or perhaps two. In a trump contract you might have several possible lines for success. Your task will be to choose the one with the best chance.

In this book, Australian expert Ron Klinger shows you how to win more often. You should feel considerable satisfaction in finding the right approach to make the number of tricks needed for your contract. In this book that satisfaction should be increased when you realize that some of the world's best players did not do as well as you.

Ron Klinger is a leading international bridge teacher and has represented Australia in eighteen world championships since 1976, including each year from 2003–2011. He has written over fifty bridge books, some of which have been translated into Bulgarian, Chinese, Danish, French, Hebrew, Icelandic and Polish.

IMPROVE YOUR PLAY AT TRUMP CONTRACTS

Ron Klinger

Weidenfeld & Nicolson
IN ASSOCIATION WITH
PETER CRAWLEY

First published in Great Britain 2012
in association with Peter Crawley
by Weidenfeld & Nicolson
a division of the Orion Publishing Group Ltd
Orion House, 5 Upper St Martin's Lane, London, WC2H 9EA

an Hachette UK Company

1 3 5 7 9 10 8 6 4 2

A catalogue record for this book
is available from the British Library.

ISBN 978 0 297 86587 2

Typeset by Modern Bridge Publications
P.O. Box 140, Northbridge NSW 1560, Australia

Printed in Great Britain by
Clays Ltd, St Ives plc

The Orion Publishing Group's policy is to use papers that are natural, renewable
and recyclable products and made from wood grown in sustainable forests.
The logging and manufacturing processes are expected to conform to the
environmental regulations of the country of origin.

www.orionbooks.co.uk

CONTENTS

Introduction

Playing a trump contract usually has more problems than one at no-trumps. Do I draw trumps or delay trumps? Is an opposition ruff threatening? Do I have enough tricks? Should I plan to ruff losers in dummy or set up a long suit? How should I manage the trump suit? Where should I win the first trick (when there is a choice)? What is the entry position in dummy and in my hand?

As always, you should try to form a plan of play before you play a card from dummy. There are several things to consider. Some habits should become automatic, regardless of the contract.

1. Count the points, those in dummy and add those in your hand. Deduct the total from 40 and you know how many points the opponents hold. If there has been any opposition bidding, you can often assess which opponent is more likely to hold a critical card.

2. Count your losers and your winners. Most textbooks and most teachers recommend that you count your losers in a trump contract and then see how to reduce them to ensure success. That is sensible advice, but it is also worthwhile counting your winners if the number is obvious. If you are in 4♠ and can see nine tricks, it is clear that you have to create an extra winner somehow.

Next you should analyse the opening lead and the information you can glean from that. Assess the likely or possible shape of the opposing hands. Once trick 1 is over, what inferences can you draw from the play by third hand?

After you have examined the possible lines of play you might adopt and which approach offers the best chance of success, consider whether any precautions are needed. Are there traps to avoid? Is the contract very likely to succeed? If so, consider how to handle bad breaks. Does the contract have little hope? Try to find a lie of the cards that will allow you to succeed.

When I first became addicted to bridge, I asked some experts of the time, how long it takes to become a really good player. The expected answer was a year, perhaps eighteen months. The general reply was, 'At least seven years'.

Why so long? Because there are so many different situations that you will need to face, you cannot come up with a sufficient representative number in a shorter period, even if you play frequently. One of the aims of this book is to give you a wider experience of declarer problems by putting you in the hot seat on deals from actual tournament play.

What do athletes do before a major competition? They train and they train and they train. Your efforts at bridge will be rewarded more often if you also train and train and train. One of the best ways of doing that is to aim to solve bridge problems regularly, whether they are on opening leads, defence or declarer play. Your game is bound to improve if you try to solve half a dozen problems every day. Also before each session of play, you should warm up, just like an athlete would, by tackling a few problems. Stimulate the brain cells and you will be ready to do battle.

All the deals come from recent major international tournaments or national championships. There are no themes and the deals do not come in any special order. At the table you have to cope with each deal on its merits. For each problem, your task is to find the best line to make your contract. Do not worry about overtricks.

Be sure to make a firm decision about the answer you would give to the problem before checking the actual solution. If your solution is not the one recommended, you can take some comfort in the fact that, in most cases, one or more top class declarers also fell from grace at the table.

All right, let's get under way.

Ron Klinger, 2012

Test Your Play

1. Dealer South : East-West vulnerable

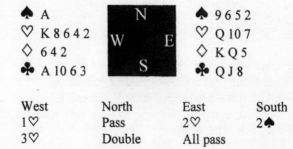

♠ A K Q 10 8 6 5
♡ A K 9
◇ 9 6
♣ A

♠ 7 3 2
♡ 10 6 3
◇ K J 10 8
♣ K 8 2

West opened 2♣ and, with no opposition bidding, West has reached 6♠.

North leads the ◇A: eight – three – six and continues with the ◇4: king – queen – nine.
Solution on page 10.

2. Dealer West : Nil vulnerable

♠ A
♡ K 8 6 4 2
◇ 6 4 2
♣ A 10 6 3

♠ 9 6 5 2
♡ Q 10 7
◇ K Q 5
♣ Q J 8

West	North	East	South
1♡	Pass	2♡	2♠
3♡	Double	All pass	

North leads the ♠7: two – ten – ace. Plan your play.
Solution on page 11.

1. Board 9, Round 1 from the 2011 World Team Championships:

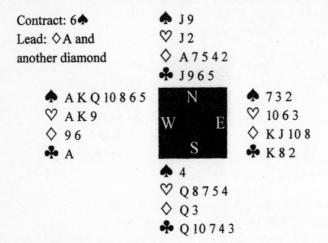

Contract: 6♠
Lead: ◇A and
another diamond

```
            ♠ J 9
            ♡ J 2
            ◇ A 7 5 4 2
            ♣ J 9 6 5
♠ AKQ10865              ♠ 7 3 2
♡ A K 9                 ♡ 10 6 3
◇ 9 6                   ◇ K J 10 8
♣ A                     ♣ K 8 2
            ♠ 4
            ♡ Q 8 7 5 4
            ◇ Q 3
            ♣ Q 10 7 4 3
```

West is in 6♠ and North leads the ◇A and another diamond. After the ◇K wins trick 2, the temptation is to draw trumps, cash the ♣A, cross to dummy with a low spade to dummy's ♠7 and discard your heart loser on one of dummy's winners.

As the cards lie, this line works, but it would fail if the missing trumps were 3-0. Now you would be unable to reach dummy.

The solution is easy enough. Play the ◇J at trick 3. South ruffs and you over-ruff. Now even if South began with all three trumps, you can draw trumps and reach dummy via the ♠7.

At some tables, after spades had been agreed and cue-bidding had revealed diamond control with East, North led a low diamond. The natural temptation is to finesse the ◇J. Peter Fredin (Sweden) and Steve Weinstein (USA) were among those who were prepared to pay North the compliment of having led away from the ◇A. They rose with dummy's ◇K and made their slam.

2. Board 11, Round 3, 2011 World Team Championships:

Contract: 3♡ doubled
Lead: ♠7

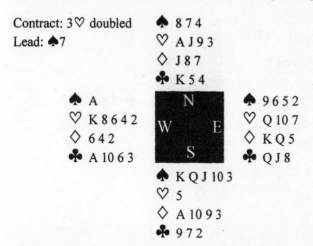

Against 3♡ doubled, North began with the ♠7: two – ten – ace. South might be false-carding, but if not, North has the ♠8 and so began with three spades. In that case North could have all the missing hearts. If North has the ◇A and South the ♣K, you have only one loser outside trumps and can afford three trump losers. If the top honours in the minor suits are in one hand you have two losers outside trumps and can afford to lose two trump tricks.

The danger position is the ♣K with North and the ◇A with South, as existed. Now, with three losers outside trumps you can afford only one trump loser. If North has the only the ♣K outside the hearts, would North really have doubled 3♡ with only ♡A-J-5-3?

That seems so unlikely that you should play North to have the ♡9. Play a low heart at trick 2. If North follows with the ♡3 (it does not help North to play the ♡9), finesse the ♡7. When that wins, take the club finesse. That loses, but you are well-placed to lose at most four tricks. In practice, West played the ♡2 at trick 2: three – ten? – five, and lost two hearts and three minor suit tricks.

3. Dealer South : Both vulnerable

♠ A Q 10 8 7 4   ♠ J 6
♡ 9 4   ♡ A K 5 3 2
◇ A J 10 5   ◇ K 7
♣ 4   ♣ A Q J 2

West opened 1♠ and, with no opposition bidding, West has ended in 6♠.

North leads the ♣10. Plan your play.
   Solution on page 14.

4. Dealer South : North-South vulnerable

♠ A J 5 2   ♠ 3
♡ 5 2   ♡ A 9 6 4 3
◇ A 6 5 4 3 2   ◇ K Q 10 7
♣ Q   ♣ A 5 4

With North-South silent, West is in 6◇. West showed diamonds and spades and East showed hearts and diamond support.

North leads the ♣J. Plan your play.
   Solution on page 15.

5. Dealer West : Both vulnerable

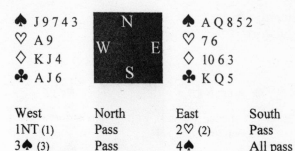

♠ J 9 7 4 3   ♠ A Q 8 5 2
♡ A 9   ♡ 7 6
◇ K J 4   ◇ 10 6 3
♣ A J 6   ♣ K Q 5

West	North	East	South
1NT (1)	Pass	2♡ (2)	Pass
3♠ (3)	Pass	4♠	All pass

(1) Ostensibly 15-17 points
(2) Transfer to spades
(3) Minimum values but excellent support

North leads the ♡2: six – jack – ace. Plan your play.

Solution on page 16.

6. Dealer West : Nil vulnerable

♠ 5   ♠ A K
♡ K Q J 10 8 4   ♡ A 7
◇ K   ◇ J 10 9 7 6 4 3
♣ K Q 7 5 2   ♣ A 6

West opened 1♡ and, with no opposition bidding, West is in 6♡.

Plan your play if:

(a) North leads the ◇A and shifts to a spade.

(b) North leads a spade.

Solution on page 17.

3. Board 13, Round 5, 2011 World Team Championships:

Contract: 6♠
Lead: ♣10

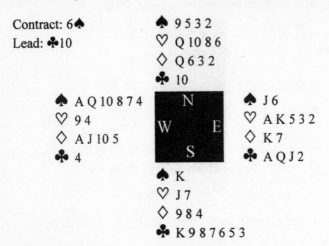

♠ 9 5 3 2
♡ Q 10 8 6
◊ Q 6 3 2
♣ 10

♠ A Q 10 8 7 4
♡ 9 4
◊ A J 10 5
♣ 4

♠ J 6
♡ A K 5 3 2
◊ K 7
♣ A Q J 2

♠ K
♡ J 7
◊ 9 8 4
♣ K 9 8 7 6 5 3

North has led the ♣10 against 6♠. There is no need to risk the club finesse at trick 1. If you have no trump loser, the slam is safe. If there is a trump loser, you have chances in hearts and diamonds to avoid a second loser. As it happens, if you do finesse in clubs at trick 1, South wins and returns a club to defeat 6♠.

You take the ♣A and start trumps. Which trump should you play first? If entries to dummy were a problem, then leading the ♠J would be best. As you have plenty of entries to dummy, you can start with the ♠6, a safety play to guard against South having the ♠K singleton. That was the actual situation. After ♠6, king, ace, you cross to the ♠J, return to the ◊A and draw trumps.

A surprising number of declarers led the ♠J at trick 2. That produced a trump loser, but recovery is possible a number of ways. You can play four rounds of trumps, win North's heart exit in dummy, play the ♣Q, king, ruff, cross to the ♡K and discard a diamond on the ♣J. North is squeezed in the red suits. Another option after trumps: run the ◊J and later squeeze North.

4. This arose in the 2011 NEC Cup, an annual event held in Japan in February, with many top overseas players invited:

Contract: 6◇
Lead: ♣J

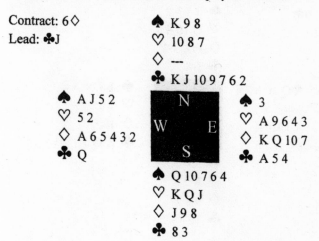

          ♠ K 9 8
          ♡ 10 8 7
          ◇ ---
          ♣ K J 10 9 7 6 2

♠ A J 5 2   ♠ 3
♡ 5 2   ♡ A 9 6 4 3
◇ A 6 5 4 3 2   ◇ K Q 10 7
♣ Q   ♣ A 5 4

          ♠ Q 10 7 6 4
          ♡ K Q J
          ◇ J 9 8
          ♣ 8 3

When North led the ♣J, declarer rose with the ♣A and played ♠A, spade ruff, club ruff, spade ruff, ♡A and a low heart. South won and continued with the ♠Q, ruffed in dummy. With three spades ruffed in dummy and trumps 3-0, West had to lose a trump trick. One off.

There is a better line of play. Take the ♣A and cash the ◇A. If trumps are 2-1, play the ♡A and give up a heart. If all follow, you can claim, as you can ruff two spades and set up a heart winner for your remaining spade loser. If trumps are 3-0, ruffing three spades will never work. Instead, play ♡A and another heart. You have to hope hearts are 3-3 (as they were).

Another option is to duck the club lead to your queen. If that wins, you have it easy. If South has the ♣K, you plan to discard a heart on the ♣A, set up the hearts and draw trumps en route. As the cards lay, ducking the club allows you to make all the tricks.

5. From the 2011 NEC Cup:

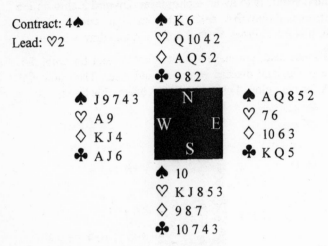

Contract: 4♠
Lead: ♡2

North led the ♡2 against 4♠. South played the ♡J to determine the location of the ♡Q. West should win with the ace and then has a choice of two competing lines:

(1) Take the spade finesse. If you decided to do this, you should start with the ♠J. This caters for the ♠K with North and in particular guards against ♠K-10-6 with North.

(2) Play a spade to the ace or lead the ♠J and go up with the ace if North follows low smoothly. If the ♠K does not drop, cash the clubs and exit with a heart. If South began with ♠K-x and the queen of diamonds, you can later endplay South to hold your diamond losers to one.

Which line is preferable? Line (1) works whenever North has the ♠K and so is a 50% chance. Line (2) requires South to hold two cards, the ♠K and the ◊Q. That makes it a worse chance than simply having the ♠K onside. After capturing the ♡J at trick 1, your best chance is to lead the ♠J at trick two and let it run if North follows low.

6. (a) West is in 6♡. After the opponents have taken a diamond, your main concern is to avoid a club loser. Discard a club on the second spade and play ♣A, ♣K. If they stand up, continue with a low club. If North follows, ruff with the ♡A and draw trumps.

(b) On a spade lead, you have a safety play to cater for clubs 5-1. Cash the spades and discard your diamond loser. Then play ♣A and duck the next club. This is the layout where this line gains:

```
              ♠ Q 9 4 3 2
              ♡ 9 6 5 2
              ◇ A Q 8
              ♣ 4
♠ 5                  N            ♠ A K
♡ K Q J 10 8 4                   ♡ A 7
◇ K           W           E      ◇ J 10 9 7 6 4 3
♣ K Q 7 5 2          S           ♣ A 6
              ♠ J 10 8 7 6
              ♡ 3
              ◇ 5 2
              ♣ J 10 9 8 3
```

If you play ♣A, ♣K after discarding your diamond loser, North ruffs and returns a trump. Now you will lose a club later to be one down. In the 2010 NEC Cup, 18 declarers in 6♡ received a spade lead and neglected the safety play in clubs. They survived their misplay and made an overtrick as the clubs were actually 4-2.

If clubs are 3-3 or 4-2, playing ♣A, ♣K and ruffing a club works 84% of the time. In 100 deals you gain 84 Imps. The chance of South having five clubs is a bit over 7%. In 100 deals failing in 6♡ when the opponents have made it costs 7 x 14 = 98 Imps not vulnerable and 7 x 17 = 119 Imps vulnerable. The additional cost is the psychological blow, not just to declarer but to the partnership.

7. Dealer West : Nil vulnerable

	♠ A K 10 8 6 2		♠ 7 4
	♡ 4 3		♡ A J 5
	◇ J		◇ A 10 8 7 2
	♣ 10 8 6 4		♣ K Q 7

West	North	East	South
2♠	Pass	2NT (1)	Pass
3♠ (2)	Pass	4♠	All pass

(1) Artificial inquiry, good hand
(2) Maximum weak two, two top honours in spades

North leads the ♡K. Plan your play.
Solution on page 20.

8. Dealer West : Nil vulnerable

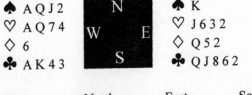

	♠ A Q J 2		♠ K
	♡ A Q 7 4		♡ J 6 3 2
	◇ 6		◇ Q 5 2
	♣ A K 4 3		♣ Q J 8 6 2

West	North	East	South
1♣	3◇	Double (1)	Pass
5NT (2)	Pass	6♣	All pass

(1) For takeout (2) Pick a slam

North leads the ◇A and shifts to the ♠5. North will
turn up with the ♣9 singleton. Plan your play.
Solution on page 21.

9. Dealer North : East-West vulnerable

♠ A 9 5
♡ A J 10 8 4
♢ 4
♣ A 8 6 5

♠ K 10 4 3
♡ 5 3 2
♢ A K 10 7
♣ 10 9

West	North	East	South
	Pass	Pass	1♠
2♡	Double (1)	2♠ (2)	Pass
4♡	Pass	Pass	Double
Pass	Pass	Pass	

(1) Both minors   (2) Strong heart raise

West leads the ♠8: three – jack – ace. Plan your play.
Solution on page 22.

10. Dealer West : Nil vulnerable

♠ 9 6 4 2
♡ K
♢ K Q 9 7 6
♣ A Q 6

♠ A Q 8 5
♡ A 8 3 2
♢ A
♣ J 8 7 5

West opened 1♢ and, with no opposition bidding,
West is in 6♠.
Plan your play if:
(a) North leads the ♣2: five – king - ace
(b) North leads the ♡5: two – nine - king
Solution on page 23.

5. From the 2010 NEC Cup:

Contract: 4♠
Lead: ♡K

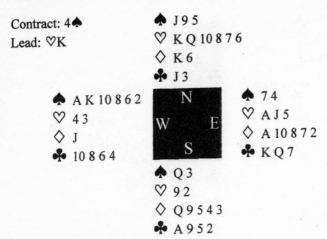

```
              ♠ J 9 5
              ♡ K Q 10 8 7 6
              ◇ K 6
              ♣ J 3
♠ A K 10 8 6 2          ♠ 7 4
♡ 4 3                   ♡ A J 5
◇ J                     ◇ A 10 8 7 2
♣ 10 8 6 4              ♣ K Q 7
              ♠ Q 3
              ♡ 9 2
              ◇ Q 9 5 4 3
              ♣ A 9 5 2
```

In one match both declarers played in 4♠ by West with no bidding by North-South. One declarer received the ♡K lead, ducked. North continued with the ♡8, won by the ♡J. To guard against South holding ♠Q-J-x-x declarer played a low spade to the ten. Call this an 'unsafety play' and West an 'unlucky expert'. North won with the ♠J and led a third heart. Dummy's ♡A was ruffed by the ♠Q. West over-ruffed, but North's ♠9 had been promoted. West thus lost two trump tricks, a heart and a club.

Sometimes easy solutions are best. Take the ♡A and play ♠A, ♠K. Then lead a heart towards dummy. This sets up the ♡J for one club discard. Later you lead a low club from hand to the ♣K. If South ducks, return to hand with a diamond ruff and lead another low club. When the ♣J falls, your contract is home.

At the other table West found a different path to self-demolition. North led the ◇K, ace. Declarer ruffed a diamond and should now play ♠A, ♠K. Instead it went club to the king, winning; low diamond, ruffed, over-ruffed; ♣J, queen, ace; club ruff. One off.

8. From qualifying Round 6, 2010 Rosenblum World Open Teams:

Contract: 6♣
Lead: ◇A
Spade switch

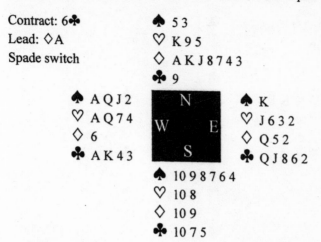

♠ 5 3
♡ K 9 5
◇ A K J 8 7 4 3
♣ 9

♠ A Q J 2   ♠ K
♡ A Q 7 4   ♡ J 6 3 2
◇ 6   ◇ Q 5 2
♣ A K 4 3   ♣ Q J 8 6 2

♠ 10 9 8 7 6 4
♡ 10 8
◇ 10 9
♣ 10 7 5

Declarer adopted this line after the ♠K won trick 2: diamond ruff; ♣A; club to the queen; ◇Q, ruffed; ♠A, ♠Q, ♠J, discarding hearts; ♡A; heart ruff; draw the last trump and claim. The problem with this line occurs when South discards a heart on the ◇Q at trick six. When declarer later plays the ♡A and a second heart, South's ♣10 is promoted.

Given North's pre-empt, the ♡K is very likely to be with South, but if you opt for the heart finesse, you would have failed in practice. You do not need to pin your hopes on that. After the ♠K wins, play a club to the ace and a club to the queen. When North shows out on the second club, North is highly unlikely to have two singletons or four hearts. Hence hearts are almost certainly 3-2.

Continue with a heart to the ace, three spades to discard three hearts from dummy, ruff a heart low, play a trump to the ♣K to draw the last trump, ruff a third heart with the ♣J and claim. This line will also succeed if South began with ♡K-x-x-x. After you discard dummy's hearts on the spades, you have a cross-ruff.

9. From qualifying Round 5, 2010 Rosenblum World Open Teams:

Contract: 4♡ doubled
Lead: ♠8

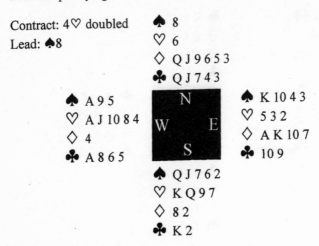

```
                    ♠ 8
                    ♡ 6
                    ◇ Q J 9 6 5 3
                    ♣ Q J 7 4 3
      ♠ A 9 5            N            ♠ K 10 4 3
      ♡ A J 10 8 4   W       E        ♡ 5 3 2
      ◇ 4                S            ◇ A K 10 7
      ♣ A 8 6 5                       ♣ 10 9
                    ♠ Q J 7 6 2
                    ♡ K Q 9 7
                    ◇ 8 2
                    ♣ K 2
```

Your side has 23 HCP, they have 17. As North must have a few points, where are South's values for the penalty double of 4♡? You can expect South to have four strong hearts or even all five hearts.

At the table declarer muffed the play. After winning trick 1, he played a low club to the ten and king. South could have beaten 4♡ at once with a spade return, but as North might have had a doubleton spade, South returned a club. West took the ace and ruffed a club. South over-ruffed and played the ♡K. Declarer lost another trick later to go two down.

West can discard club loser on the diamonds and another later on the spades. There is no need to touch clubs. At trick 2 play a diamond to the ace and cash the ◇K, pitching a club. Now lead a heart. Capture the ♡Q or ♡K and run the ♠9 to the queen. Win the club exit with the ace and cash the spades, discarding a club. Play a heart, finessing the ♡8 if South plays the ♡7. If South plays low on the first heart from dummy, you can succeed by finessing the ♡8 at once or via ♡J and a diamond later after the fourth spade.

10. From the Round of 64, 2010 Rosenblum World Open Teams:

Contract: 6♠
Lead: ♣2

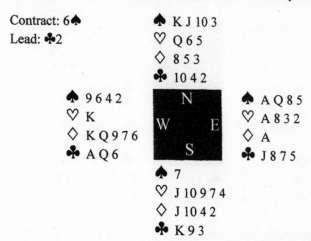

♠ K J 10 3
♡ Q 6 5
◇ 8 5 3
♣ 10 4 2

♠ 9 6 4 2
♡ K
◇ K Q 9 7 6
♣ A Q 6

♠ A Q 8 5
♡ A 8 3 2
◇ A
♣ J 8 7 5

♠ 7
♡ J 10 9 7 4
◇ J 10 4 2
♣ K 9 3

There were six declarers in 6♠. Three received a club lead to the king and ace and two were successful. Once you have no club loser, you have a safety play available in spades: lead a low spade to the eight or lead the ♠9 and let it run if North plays low. If South wins with the ♠10 or ♠J, you plan to finesse the ♠Q later. This gains, as opposed to a spade to the queen at trick 2, when North has ♠J-10-x or ♠K-J-10-x.

Fulvio Fantoni (Italy) ran the ♠9 and continued with a spade to the queen. When that won, he cashed the ♠A and claimed. Jean-Michel Voldoire (France) played a low spade to the eight, returned to the ♡K and played a spade to the queen. The rest was routine.

The other three in 6♠ received a heart lead. Although 6♠ can be made double dummy, the temptation is to avoid risking the club finesse. You plan to set up an extra trick in diamonds and discard dummy's club losers on the diamonds. A normal line, failing here, is finesse the ♠Q; cash ♠A; cash ◇A; ruff a heart; cash the ◇K, ◇Q; ruff a diamond; ruff a heart and play the fifth diamond. This line works when North has ♠K-x-x and diamonds are 4-3.

11. Dealer South : Both vulnerable

♠ 10 4		♠ 6	
♡ A 2	N	♡ K J 9	
◇ K J 6	W E	◇ A Q 8 7 5 2	
♣ A J 10 7 5 4	S	♣ K 9 3	

West	North	East	South
			Pass
1♣	Pass	1◇	Double
2♣	2♠	4♣	4♠
5♣	Pass	6♣	All pass

North leads the ♠A and shifts to the ♡6: nine – queen – ace.
Plan your play.

Solution on page 26.

12. Dealer South : Nil vulnerable

♠ 4		♠ K J 9 8	
♡ Q 10 6 5 3	N	♡ A K 8	
◇ A 10 3	W E	◇ K 8 4 2	
♣ A Q J 2	S	♣ 8 4	

After an auction in which you take no great pride, you
are West in 6♡. North leads the ♠A and continues
with the ♠3. Plan your play.

Solution on page 27.

13. Dealer East : Nil vulnerable

♠ A Q J 9 3	♠ 6
♡ 7	♡ A K J 8 4 2
◊ A K Q 5 4 3	◊ 10 7
♣ A	♣ Q J 10 5

With no opposition bidding, West has reached 6◊.

North leads the ♣4: five – nine – ace. Plan your play.
Solution on page 28.

14. Dealer South : Both vulnerable

♠ K	♠ A Q 10 9 7 6
♡ A K 3	♡ 8
◊ A 6 3	◊ Q J 10 9
♣ A K 7 5 3 2	♣ 9 8

With no opposition bidding, West has reached 6♣.

West leads the ♡5: eight – ten – ace. Plan your play.
Solution on page 29.

11. From the 2011 Asia-Pacific Teams:

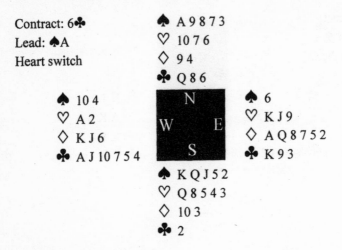

Contract: 6♣
Lead: ♠A
Heart switch

♠ A 9 8 7 3
♡ 10 7 6
◊ 9 4
♣ Q 8 6

♠ 10 4
♡ A 2
◊ K J 6
♣ A J 10 7 5 4

♠ 6
♡ K J 9
◊ A Q 8 7 5 2
♣ K 9 3

♠ K Q J 5 2
♡ Q 8 5 4 3
◊ 10 3
♣ 2

Unless you have good reasons to the contrary, the normal play in clubs is to play the king and ace. A number of declarers failed in 6♣ and perhaps they had no strong clues as to the trump position.

After the auction given, there is a case to place the ♣Q with North. South, a passed hand, has doubled for takeout and then competed to 4♠ after North bid only 2♠. South will be short in both minors, perhaps even a singleton in each. Therefore cash the ♣A and continue with the ♣J, letting it run if North plays low. This does not come with guarantees, but it figures to be the best chance.

Why not take a first-round finesse in clubs, leading the jack at once without cashing the ace first? That caters for North having all four clubs as well as ♣Q-x-x. Not only might the first-round finesse lose to the bare queen with South, but there is a very good reason why North is unlikely to have four clubs. With all the missing trumps, North would have continued spades at trick 2 to try to force dummy to ruff and thus ensure a trump trick.

12. From the semi-finals, 2010 Rosenblum World Open Teams:

Contract: 6♡
Lead: ♠A
Then the ♠3

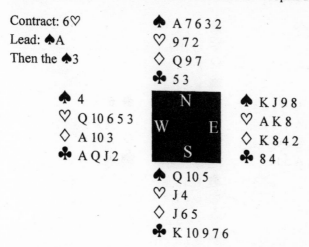

```
                    ♠ A 7 6 3 2
                    ♡ 9 7 2
                    ◇ Q 9 7
                    ♣ 5 3
   ♠ 4                            ♠ K J 9 8
   ♡ Q 10 6 5 3        N          ♡ A K 8
   ◇ A 10 3        W       E      ◇ K 8 4 2
   ♣ A Q J 2           S          ♣ 8 4
                    ♠ Q 10 5
                    ♡ J 4
                    ◇ J 6 5
                    ♣ K 10 9 7 6
```

At three tables the contract was 4♡. The remaining table reached 6♡ on the ♠A lead, followed by the ♠3. At trick 2 declarer played the ♠8, ten, ♡3. Then came heart to the ace; club finesse; heart to the king; club finesse. When West continued with the ♣2, North ruffed with the ♡9 to put 6♡ one down.

The slam is not very good, but it was a shame to fail when the club finesse was working and trumps were 3-2. There are various ways to come to 12 tricks. This one is as easy as any: take the ♠K at trick 2, discarding a diamond; finesse in clubs; play a heart to the ace; repeat the club finesse; play the ♣2. If North ruffs, you over-ruff and play a trump. If North does not ruff, you ruff low, cash the ♡K, cross to the ◇A and draw the last trump.

If North had only two clubs and ♡J-9-2 and ruffs the third club with the ♡9, you over-ruff with the ♡K. Now on the ♡8, South follows low and West has to guess the position. Still, if the layout is like that, the actual line chosen would still have failed.

13. From the 2010 World Bridge Series:

Contract: 6◇
Lead: ♣4

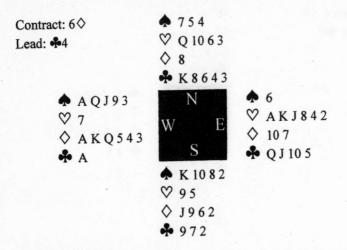

♠ 754
♡ Q 10 6 3
◇ 8
♣ K 8 6 4 3

♠ A Q J 9 3
♡ 7
◇ A K Q 5 4 3
♣ A

♠ 6
♡ A K J 8 4 2
◇ 10 7
♣ Q J 10 5

♠ K 10 8 2
♡ 9 5
◇ J 9 6 2
♣ 9 7 2

Two of the world's top declarers were among those who went down in this slam. After winning trick 1, they played ◇A, ◇K and found there was a trump loser. They continued with the ◇Q, heart to the jack and two spades were discarded on the ♡A, ♡K. Even with the ♠K onside, declarer could not escape a spade loser.

Chris Willenken (USA) made the slam without the need to take any finesse. After taking the ♣A, he played ♠A and ruffed a spade. He followed up with club ruff, spade ruff, club ruff. He was down to ◇A-K-Q-5 in trumps and played off the top three. He crossed to the ♡A, cashed the ♡K, discarding a spade and now had only the A-Q left in spades, plus the ◇5. South had the ♠K-10 and the ◇J.

When West played another heart from dummy, South was stymied. If he ruffed, West would discard the ♠Q. If South pitched a spade, West would ruff with his last trump and cash the ♠A. Either way West had twelve tricks.

14. From the 2010 World Seniors' Teams:

Contract: 6♣
Lead: ♡5

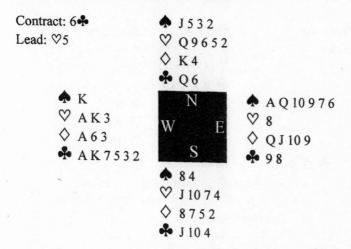

♠ J 5 3 2
♡ Q 9 6 5 2
♢ K 4
♣ Q 6

♠ K
♡ A K 3
♢ A 6 3
♣ A K 7 5 3 2

♠ A Q 10 9 7 6
♡ 8
♢ Q J 10 9
♣ 9 8

♠ 8 4
♡ J 10 7 4
♢ 8 7 5 2
♣ J 10 4

You should assume that clubs are 3-2. You have far too much work to do to try to cater for a 4-1 break. There are three feasible lines:

(1) Take the ♡A, play the ♡K and ruff the ♡3, followed by the ♣A, ♣K and ♠K. Exit with the third club. If North wins and has no more hearts, you are home. If South wins and is out of hearts, South will switch to a diamond and you will need the diamond finesse. However, if the player with the third club has a heart you are almost certainly doomed.

(2) Play ♡A, ♡K, heart ruff, ♣A, ♣K and a third club. Ruff the likely heart return, overtake the ♠K in dummy and cash the ♠A. You are home if the ♠J has dropped. If not, finesse in diamonds.

(3) Take the ♡A, cash the ♣A and ♠K, play the ♡K and ruff the ♡3. Continue with the ♠A and the ♠Q, discarding your diamond losers. You succeed whenever the spades are 3-3 and also when they are 4-2 if the hand ruffing the third spade is the opponent who began with three trumps. This line has the best chance.

15. Dealer North : North-South vulnerable

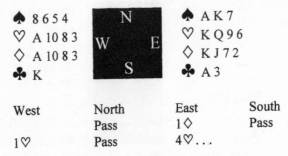

♠ 8654
♡ A 10 8 3
♢ A 10 8 3
♣ K

♠ A K 7
♡ K Q 9 6
♢ K J 7 2
♣ A 3

West	North	East	South
	Pass	1♢	Pass
1♡	Pass	4♡ . . .	

West checked on key cards and ended in 6♡.
North leads the ♡2: six – jack – ace. Plan your play.
  Solution on page 32.

16. Dealer East : North-South vulnerable

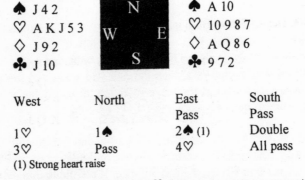

♠ J 4 2
♡ A K J 5 3
♢ J 9 2
♣ J 10

♠ A 10
♡ 10 9 8 7
♢ A Q 8 6
♣ 9 7 2

West	North	East	South
		Pass	Pass
1♡	1♠	2♠ (1)	Double
3♡	Pass	4♡	All pass

(1) Strong heart raise

East should have passed 3♡, but some partners cannot
be restrained. North leads the ♠6: ace – five – two.
North-South play low-encouraging. You play a heart to
the ace and North drops the queen. When you cash the
♡K, ♡J, North discards two spades. Plan your play.
  Solution on page 33.

17. Dealer North : Nil vulnerable

♠ K J 9 3
♡ A Q 10 9
♦ Q 4
♣ A 10 4

♠ A 10 8 7 5
♡ 3
♦ J 7
♣ Q J 7 6 2

West	North	East	South
	Pass	Pass	Pass
1NT	Pass	2♡ (1)	Pass
3♣ (2)	Pass	3♡ (3)	Pass
3♠	Pass	4♠	All pass

(1) Transfer to spades   (2) Spade support, long suit trial bid
(3) Re-transfer to spades

North plays ♦A, ♦K and then the ♡7. Plan your play
Solution on page 34.

18. Dealer West : Both vulnerable

♠ K J 8 7 2
♡ 10 7
♦ K J 10
♣ A 10 8

♠ 10 6 5 4
♡ A Q 6
♦ 9 5
♣ K Q J 7

West	North	East	South
1♠	1NT (1)	Double	Redble (2)
Pass	2♦	4♠	All pass

(1) 15-18 points, at least one spade stopper
(2) Rescue redouble

North leads the ♣4. Plan your play.
Solution on page 35.

15. From the 2011 Asia-Pacific Teams:

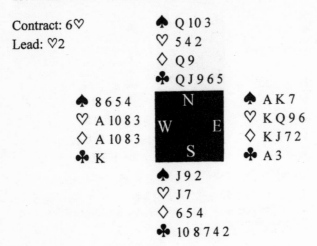

Contract: 6♡
Lead: ♡2

```
              ♠ Q 10 3
              ♡ 5 4 2
              ◊ Q 9
              ♣ Q J 9 6 5
♠ 8 6 5 4         N          ♠ A K 7
♡ A 10 8 3                   ♡ K Q 9 6
◊ A 10 8 3    W       E      ◊ K J 7 2
♣ K               S          ♣ A 3
              ♠ J 9 2
              ♡ J 7
              ◊ 6 5 4
              ♣ 10 8 7 4 2
```

In the Open, five declarers made 6♡ and two failed. One of the declarers who failed received a trump lead. He captured South's ♡J, played a heart to the king, a club to the king and a heart to the queen. He cashed the ♣A, discarding a spade from hand. This was an error. He continued with the ♠A, ♠K and a third spade. The plan was to endplay the opponents into opening up the diamond suit. North-South knew that declarer had four diamonds and so they gave him a useless ruff-and-discard. West still had to find the ◊Q and when he misguessed he was one down.

In the Seniors ten declarers were in 6♡. Seven were successful. Peter Buchen of Australia received the ♣Q lead and showed how the hand should be played. After the ♣K won, West drew trumps, ♡A, ♡K, ♡Q. On the ♣A he discarded a *diamond* and then came the ♠A, ♠K and a third spade. It did not matter which opponent won the third spade. A diamond exit would solve that problem and so would a ruff-and-discard. If it turned out spades were not 3-3, then declarer could try to pick the diamond position.

16. From the 2011 Asia-Pacific Teams:

Contract: 4♡
Lead: ♠6

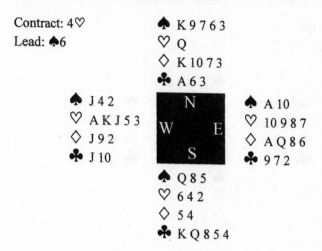

♠ K 9 7 6 3
♡ Q
◇ K 10 7 3
♣ A 6 3

♠ J 4 2
♡ A K J 5 3
◇ J 9 2
♣ J 10

♠ A 10
♡ 10 9 8 7
◇ A Q 8 6
♣ 9 7 2

♠ Q 8 5
♡ 6 4 2
◇ 5 4
♣ K Q 8 5 4

When you are in a rotten contract, all is forgiven by team-mates if you make it. They are not forgiving when you bid to an awful game and fail when you could have made it on a reasonable line.

West took the ♠A and cashed three hearts. Next came a low diamond to the queen. That won, but the contract could no longer be made since West had to lose a diamond, a spade and two clubs.

Playing North for ◇K-x was a poor chance. With a singleton heart, North was more likely to have diamond length than shortage. With three losers in the black suits, West cannot afford to lose a diamond. As you must assume North has the ◇K you should start by leading the ◇J. If North fails to cover, you have it easy.

North should play the ◇K, taken by the ace. You exit with a club. When you regain the lead, play the ◇9 and let it run. If diamonds are 3-3, the only hope is the second finesse. If North has four diamonds and South two, there are four 10-x doubletons, but six doubletons without the ten. The odds strongly favour taking the second diamond finesse rather than hoping for 10-x with South.

17. From a National Butler Trials, 2011 (pairs scored by Imps):

Contract: 4♠
Lead: ◇A, ◇K

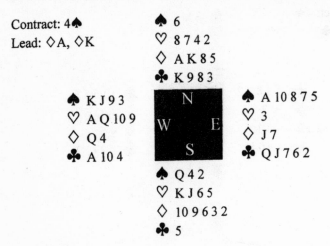

```
                      ♠ 6
                      ♡ 8 7 4 2
                      ◇ A K 8 5
                      ♣ K 9 8 3
    ♠ K J 9 3                        ♠ A 10 8 7 5
    ♡ A Q 10 9                       ♡ 3
    ◇ Q 4                            ◇ J 7
    ♣ A 10 4                         ♣ Q J 7 6 2
                      ♠ Q 4 2
                      ♡ K J 6 5
                      ◇ 10 9 6 3 2
                      ♣ 5
```

Every table (31 Open, 21 Women's) played in 4♠. In the Open, 11
Wests were declarer (seven made it) and 20 Easts (11 successful).
Datum: N-S 230. In the Women's five Wests were declarer, all on
a top diamond lead. Only one made it. Of the 16 Easts in 4♠,
eight were successful.

When West is declarer it is hard for North to avoid the tell-tale
start of ◇A, ◇K. North, a passed hand has shown up with 7 HCP.
North will not hold both the ♠Q and the ♣K. That would be 12
points, too much for a passed hand. Therefore you should play
♠A and then finesse the ♠J. On the actual layout that wins, but
had it lost, you can be confident that the ♣K will be with South.

At one table East opened a weak 2♠ (five spades, 5-minor) in
second seat and West raised to 4♠. South led the ♡5, taken by the
ace. Declarer played ♠K, ♠A and that was one down. Can it hurt
to play a diamond at trick 2? If you discover that North has ◇K,
◇A, you now know enough to take the spade finesse against South.

18. From the finals of three National Teams' events in 2011:

Contract: 4♠
Lead: ♣4

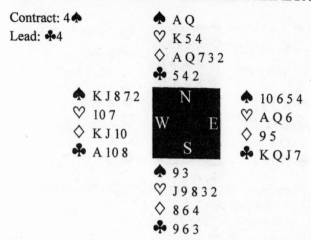

         ♠ A Q
         ♡ K 5 4
         ◇ A Q 7 3 2
         ♣ 5 4 2

♠ K J 8 7 2   ♠ 10 6 5 4
♡ 10 7   ♡ A Q 6
◇ K J 10   ◇ 9 5
♣ A 10 8   ♣ K Q J 7

         ♠ 9 3
         ♡ J 9 8 3 2
         ◇ 8 6 4
         ♣ 9 6 3

Four tables played in 4♠. One was successful. Counting points will clarify the position. You have 12 HCP, so has dummy. Total 24. Of the 16 HCP, North will have almost every one, since North has overcalled 1NT, 15-18 points. You can thus place North with the ♡K and with the A-Q in spades and in diamonds.

Since you are faced with two spade losers and two diamond losers you have to hope that an endplay on North will succeed. Win the club lead in hand and finesse ♡Q. Cash the ♡A and ruff the third heart. Then play the ♣A and a club to the king. If you have survived to this point, with clubs 3-3, play a spade to the jack.

With the actual layout North can take two spades, but then has to lead a diamond. That means you will lose only one diamond trick. Even if North started with a 2-4-4-3 pattern and plays a heart after taking two spades, a ruff-and-discard allows you to throw a diamond from dummy and you still succeed.

19. Dealer West : Both vulnerable

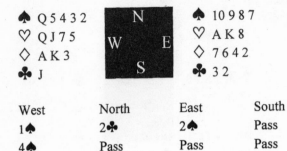

♠ Q 5 4 3 2
♡ Q J 7 5
◇ A K 3
♣ J

♠ 10 9 8 7
♡ A K 8
◇ 7 6 4 2
♣ 3 2

West	North	East	South
1♠	2♣	2♠	Pass
4♠	Pass	Pass	Pass

North leads the ♣A, followed by the ♣K, which you ruff. Plan your play.

Solution on page 38.

20. Dealer North : Nil vulnerable

♠ K 3
♡ A K J 10 9 5
◇ 7 3
♣ 9 6 5

♠ A Q J 8 7
♡ 4 2
◇ A K Q J 9
♣ 7

West	North	East	South
	Pass	1♠	Pass
2♡	Pass	3◇	Pass
3♡	Pass	4♡	Pass
4NT	Pass	5♡ (1)	All pass

(1) Two key cards for hearts, no ♡Q.

North leads the ♣A. How would you play if:
(a) North switches to the ♠2?
(b) North continues with ♣3?

Solution on page 39.

21. Dealer North : Nil vulnerable

	♠ J 4 3		♠ A 9 8 6 5 2
	♡ A J 4 3		♡ 10 9
	◇ K 9 7 5		◇ A 6 3
	♣ A K		♣ J 9

West	North	East	South
	Pass	Pass	1♡
1NT	2♡	4◇ (1)	Pass
4♠	Pass	Pass	Pass

(1) Transfer to spades

(a) North leads the ♡8: nine – queen - ace. Plan your play.

(b) How would you play if there had been no opposition bidding and North leads a club?

Solution on page 40.

22. Dealer West : North-South vulnerable

	♠ Q 8 4		♠ A 10 6 2
	♡ J 4		♡ A K
	◇ A K Q J 9 5 4		◇ 10 7 3 2
	♣ J		♣ A 10 6

West	North	East	South
1◇	Dble	1♠	Pass
3◇	Pass	4NT	Pass
5♠ (1)	Pass	6◇	All pass

(1) Two key cards for diamonds and the ◇Q

North leads the ♣K. Plan your play.

Solution on page 41.

19. From the 2011 Asia-Pacific Teams:

Contract: 4♠
Lead: ♣A, ♣K

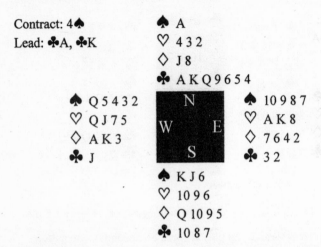

♠ A
♡ 4 3 2
◇ J 8
♣ A K Q 9 6 5 4

♠ Q 5 4 3 2
♡ Q J 7 5
◇ A K 3
♣ J

♠ 10 9 8 7
♡ A K 8
◇ 7 6 4 2
♣ 3 2

♠ K J 6
♡ 10 9 6
◇ Q 10 9 5
♣ 10 8 7

Declarer ruffed the ♣K and feebly led a trump. He lost two spades and, in due course, a diamond for one down. Having lost one club and bound to lose two spades, you must eliminate the diamond loser. To that end, you need a ruff-and-discard. You must play North for only two diamonds and either the ♠A bare or ♠A-K doubleton. The hopes are slim, but there is no other chance.

Play ◇A, ◇K, ♡A, ♡K and ♡Q. Now exit with a spade. On the above layout, North wins and has only clubs left. You ruff the club exit in dummy, discarding your diamond loser and lead a spade. You lose only two spades and a club.

North can foil you by cashing the ♠A before the second club. The above line also works if North is 2-2-2-7 with ♠A-K doubleton and does not cash the spades before playing the second club.

On the actual deal North had ♠K bare, not ♠A bare. West should follow the same line, but when West exits with a spade, South can defeat you by overtaking North's ♠K and playing a diamond. Still, players do not always do the right thing.

20. From the 2011 Asia-Pacific Teams:

Contract: 5♡
Lead: ♣A

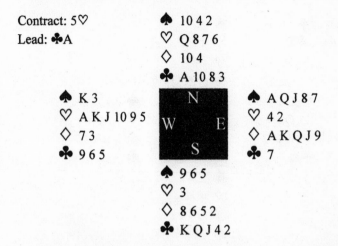

- ♠ 10 4 2
- ♡ Q 8 7 6
- ◊ 10 4
- ♣ A 10 8 3

- ♠ K 3
- ♡ A K J 10 9 5
- ◊ 7 3
- ♣ 9 6 5

- ♠ A Q J 8 7
- ♡ 4 2
- ◊ A K Q J 9
- ♣ 7

- ♠ 9 6 5
- ♡ 3
- ◊ 8 6 5 2
- ♣ K Q J 4 2

(a) One North switched to the ♠2 at trick 2. Declarer won with the ♠K, ruffed a club and played ♡A, ♡K. As a third heart would be fatal, West played ◊A, ◊K, ♠A. He then had to guess which winner to play to discard the club loser. Not trusting North's carding, West played a third diamond. North ruffed low. One off.

West should win trick 2 with the ♠A and take the heart finesse. If North takes the ♡Q, West can win any return, come to hand with the ♠K, draw trumps and claim. If North ducks, ruff a club, play ♠K, ♡A, ♡K and then ◊A, ◊K and any winner from dummy to pitch a club. North can ruff with the ♡Q, but West has the rest.

(b) When North continues clubs at trick 2, you ruff, but you cannot afford the heart finesse. Cross to the ♠K and ruff your third club. Cash ◊A, ◊K, ♠A to create a safe return to hand and prevent any chance of a trump promotion for North. Then ruff a spade or a diamond with the ♡J. If North over-ruffs, win any return and draw trumps. If North does not over-ruff, continue with ♡A, ♡K and the ♡10. North cannot prevent 11 tricks.

21. From a National Open Team Selection Trials:

Contract: 4♠
Lead: ♡8

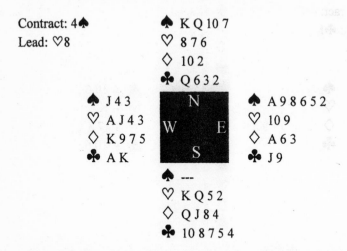

```
                        ♠ K Q 10 7
                        ♡ 8 7 6
                        ♢ 10 2
                        ♣ Q 6 3 2
        ♠ J 4 3              N           ♠ A 9 8 6 5 2
        ♡ A J 4 3        W       E       ♡ 10 9
        ♢ K 9 7 5            S           ♢ A 6 3
        ♣ A K                           ♣ J 9
                        ♠ ---
                        ♡ K Q 5 2
                        ♢ Q J 8 4
                        ♣ 10 8 7 5 4
```

(a) As you have no club losers and can give up a heart to create a winner to eliminate dummy's diamond loser, you simply have to avoid losing three trump tricks. This is quite simple: play a low spade and if North plays the ♠7, cover with the ♠8. If that loses, the ♠A later will give the defence two trump tricks at most. On the actual layout the ♠8 wins. It does not help North to insert the ♠10. Take the ♠A, play a spade to the jack and eventually draw North's last trump. At the table West led the ♠J at trick 2. That worked, but it could have looked silly if South was the one with four spades, perhaps with a 4-4-2-3 pattern.

(b) On a club lead you should play the same way: low spade, seven, eight from dummy. You plan to take two heart finesses to take care of dummy's diamond loser. Your entries are the ♠A and ♢A. As diamonds have not been attacked yet, there is no urgency to take the ♠A on the first round. You can afford the safety play of ducking a spade. It will not hurt if spades are 2-2 or 3-1 and caters for the 4-0.

22. From the 2010 Buffet Cup, Europe vs USA:

Contract: 6◇
Lead: ♣K

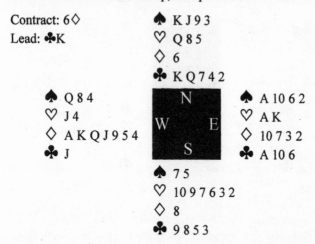

```
                    ♠ K J 9 3
                    ♡ Q 8 5
                    ◇ 6
                    ♣ K Q 7 4 2
  ♠ Q 8 4                              ♠ A 10 6 2
  ♡ J 4                                ♡ A K
  ◇ A K Q J 9 5 4                      ◇ 10 7 3 2
  ♣ J                                  ♣ A 10 6
                    ♠ 7 5
                    ♡ 10 9 7 6 3 2
                    ◇ 8
                    ♣ 9 8 5 3
```

You can see 11 tricks and need to create one extra trick. If you play ♠A and another spade at some stage you will fail. If you lead a low spade to the ten, that will work. Similarly, you can draw trumps, cross to dummy and play a low spade to the queen. That loses, but you can finesse the ♠10 later for success. Both of those lines require North to hold the ♠J. That is quite likely, but not certain. If South happened to have the ♠J, you would fail.

Fred Gitelman (USA) made the slam regardless of the position of the ♠J. All he needed was for North to have the ♠K and the ♣Q, virtual certainties on the bidding and the opening lead. He ducked the opening lead! North switched to a heart. West drew trumps, cashed the ♣A and the other heart and ran his diamond winners. With one trump to go East had ♠A-10 ♣10, North ♠K-J ♣Q and West ♠Q-8 ◇4. When the last diamond was played, North discarded the ♠J, dummy the ♣10. Then came the ♠8, king, ace and the ♠Q was West's twelfth trick.

23. Dealer South : North-South vulnerable

♠ K 10 9 5 3		♠ A 4 2
♡ A K 10 2	N	♡ 8 5
◇ 8 6	W E	◇ Q 9 4
♣ 9 4	S	♣ A K J 8 7

West	North	East	South
			Pass
Pass	Pass	1♣	Pass
1♠	Pass	2♠	Pass
4♠	Pass	Pass	Pass

North leads the ◇A, then the ◇5: queen – king. South
plays the ◇J. You ruff and North over-ruffs. North shifts
to the ♣2. Which trump did you play at trick 3?
Plan your play from here.
  Solution on page 44.

24. Dealer West : Nil vulnerable

♠ 5 4		♠ K Q 9
♡ K Q 10 7	N	♡ A 8 4 2
◇ J 10 8 6	W E	◇ A Q 4
♣ K Q 2	S	♣ 9 5 4

West	North	East	South
Pass	Pass	1♣	Pass
1♡	Pass	2♡	Pass
4♡	Pass	Pass	Pass

North leads the ◇5. Plan your play.
  Solution on page 45.

25. Dealer West : Nil vulnerable

♠ K Q 7		♠ 9 6 2
♡ A 7 4 2		♡ K J 9 3
◇ A K J 7		◇ Q 6 5
♣ Q J		♣ 7 6 3

West	North	East	South
1◇	1♠	Dble	Pass
4♡	Pass	Pass	Pass

North leads the ♣K: three – four – jack, followed by the ♣2: six – ace – queen. South switches to the ♠8: king – ace – two and North returns the ♠J: six – five – queen. West plays the ♡A: five – three – ten from South. Next the ♡2, six from North . . .

Which heart do you play from dummy? Why?

Solution on page 46.

26. Dealer South : East-West vulnerable

♠ Q 9		♠ A 7 6 5 3
♡ 10 9 5 3		♡ J 8 6 2
◇ A Q J 9		◇ 10
♣ A K 6		♣ Q 10 3

West opened 1NT and a Stayman auction ended in 4♡ by West. North leads the ♣2. Where do you win this?

At trick 2 you play a low heart, won by North with the ♡K, South playing the ♡7. North continues with a club.

Plan your play.

Solution on page 47.

23. From Australia vs New Zealand Open Teams 2005:

Contract: 4♠
Lead: ◇A

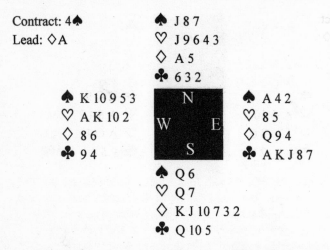

```
                    ♠ J 8 7
                    ♡ J 9 6 4 3
                    ◇ A 5
                    ♣ 6 3 2
  ♠ K 10 9 5 3              ♠ A 4 2
  ♡ A K 10 2               ♡ 8 5
  ◇ 8 6                    ◇ Q 9 4
  ♣ 9 4                    ♣ A K J 8 7
                    ♠ Q 6
                    ♡ Q 7
                    ◇ K J 10 7 3 2
                    ♣ Q 10 5
```

At both tables the play began with three rounds of diamonds, West ruffing low, over-ruffed, and North exiting with a low club, taken by the ace. The New Zealand declarer played ♠A, ♠K. As North had five cards in spades and diamonds to South's eight cards, West placed North with the club length and finessed the ♣J, in case North had started with ♣Q-x-x-x. That was one down.

The Australian West took the ♣A at trick 4 and continued with the ♣K and a low club. With clubs 3-3 he was home. He would also be all right if North had started with ♣Q-x-x-x. He could ruff the third club, play ♠K, ♠A, ruff the fourth club, cash ♡A, ♡K, ruff a heart and pitch the other heart on dummy's club winner.

It is certainly reasonable to ruff the third diamond with the ♠10 or ♠9. North still over-ruffs and the play proceeds as above. Then, after ♣A, ♣K, third club, if South is out of clubs and ruffs, West can comfortably over-ruff. If West ruffs the third diamond low, as happened, and South can ruff the third club later with the ♠Q, West will need to guess the trump layout.

24. From a National Swiss Pairs, scored by Imps, 2007:

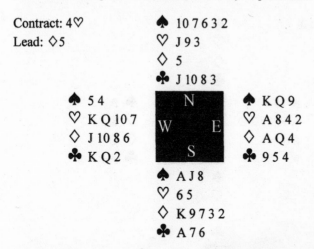

Contract: 4♡
Lead: ◊5

North:
♠ 10 7 6 3 2
♡ J 9 3
◊ 5
♣ J 10 8 3

West:
♠ 5 4
♡ K Q 10 7
◊ J 10 8 6
♣ K Q 2

East:
♠ K Q 9
♡ A 8 4 2
◊ A Q 4
♣ 9 5 4

South:
♠ A J 8
♡ 6 5
◊ K 9 7 3 2
♣ A 7 6

Declarer should rise with the ◊A and draw trumps. If trumps are 3-2, the contract is safe. After drawing trumps, play a diamond to the queen and knock out the ◊K. One of dummy's clubs goes away on the fourth diamond. You lose only three tricks.

Declarer erred by taking the diamond finesse. South won and returned the ◊2, suit-preference for clubs. A club to the ace was followed by another diamond ruff. West still had to lose to the ♠A and that meant two down in a cold contract.

What if you go up with the ◊A and find that the trumps are 4-1, with the ◊K onside all along? The chance of trumps 3-2 is about 68%, trumps 4-1 28%. Is North more likely to be leading a singleton or leading away from the ◊K? Leading from a king-high suit is not particularly attractive, but leading a singleton is, especially from a really weak hand.

Consider your feelings afterwards (and partner's). Will you feel worse if you rise with the ◊A and trumps are 4-1 or will you feel worse if you finesse at trick 1 and suffer two ruffs?

25. From a 2011 National Open Butler Trials, scored by Imps:

Contract: 4♡
Lead: ♣K

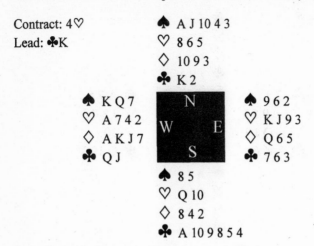

North led the ♣K and continued with the ♣2 to the ace. South switched to the ♠8, king, ace, and North returned the ♠J, taken by the queen. West cashed the ♡A and South played the ♡10. On the next heart North followed low. Up with the ♡K or finesse ♡J?

The normal play with this combination is to finesse the jack on the second round. South's ♡10 could be a false card from ♡10-x to try to fool you into rejecting the finesse. In addition, North is the one who bid and so is more likely to have strength, hence the ♡Q. Therefore you need a very strong reason to play the ♡K here.

South has in fact given you the very good reason. North's club play has indicated a doubleton. In fact, a third club would defeat 4♡. Why then did South not play a third club? The shift to spades was surprising. The answer is that South was afraid that West would probably have the ♡8 and would ruff the third club with it. That would then give away the location of the ♡Q. You should play the ♡K, draw the last trump and pitch a spade on the fourth diamond.

26. From the 2011 World Team Championships, Round 7, Board 3:

Contract: 4♡
Lead: ♣2

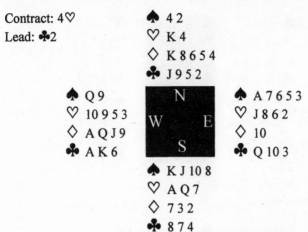

```
              ♠ 4 2
              ♡ K 4
              ◊ K 8 6 5 4
              ♣ J 9 5 2
   ♠ Q 9            N          ♠ A 7 6 5 3
   ♡ 10 9 5 3    W     E       ♡ J 8 6 2
   ◊ A Q J 9                   ◊ 10
   ♣ A K 6          S          ♣ Q 10 3
              ♠ K J 10 8
              ♡ A Q 7
              ◊ 7 3 2
              ♣ 8 7 4
```

The defence can always defeat 4♡, but what is clear to declarer is not always clear to the defence. Your task is to give the defence tough decisions. Then, if they misfire, you need to envisage a position where your contract can succeed.

Bill Haughie of Australia did just that on this deal. He took trick 1 with the ♣Q in dummy in order to make it obvious that a club continuation was perfectly safe. Next came the ♡2: seven – ten – king. This was the critical moment for North. A spade switch or a heart return would defeat 4♡, but North continued with the 'safe' club. That was all that declarer needed.

He played ◊A, then ◊J, ducked, followed by the ◊Q, covered by the ◊K and ruffed. After a club to hand West played the ◊9. South discarded, but there was no salvation. West led a heart. South won and could cash the other heart winner, but then had to lead a spade, allowing West to score the ♠Q. West needed to visualize a situation where a defender with the ♠K would be forced to win the second round of hearts and have no safe exit.

27. Dealer North : East-West vulnerable

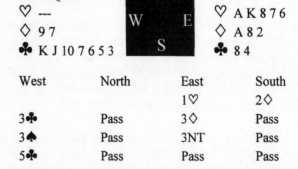

♠ 9 4   N   ♠ A K 7 2
♡ A K Q 2   W   E   ♡ 8 7 5 3
◇ A K 9 8   ◇ 10 2
♣ A 5 3   S   ♣ K 7 4

West	North	East	South
	Pass	Pass	Pass
2NT	Pass	3♣ (1)	Pass
3♡	Pass	4NT	Pass
5◇ (2)	Pass	6♡	All pass

(1) Simple Stayman   (2) 1 or 4 key cards, obviously four

North leads the ♠5. Plan your play.
    Solution on page 50.

28. Dealer East : North-South vulnerable

♠ A Q 5 2   N   ♠ 8 7 3
♡ ---   W   E   ♡ A K 8 7 6
◇ 9 7   ◇ A 8 2
♣ K J 10 7 6 5 3 S   ♣ 8 4

West	North	East	South
		1♡	2◇
3♣	Pass	3◇	Pass
3♠	Pass	3NT	Pass
5♣	Pass	Pass	Pass

North leads the ◇J. You take the ◇A and pitch a diamond
and a spade on the ♡A, ♡K. What next? If you choose the
♣4 South plays the ♣9. Which club do you play from hand?
    Solution on page 51.

29. Dealer East : Both vulnerable

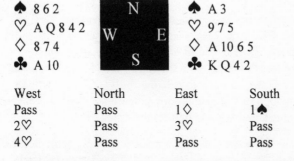

♠ K Q 5 3
♡ A
♢ A K Q 8 5
♣ 9 8 3

♠ J 9 4
♡ 9 8 7
♢ 10 9 7 4
♣ 10 5 2

West	North	East	South
		Pass	Pass
1◇	1♡	Pass	3♡ (1)
Double	Pass	4◇	All pass

(1) Pre-emptive, 6-9 points

North leads the ♡3: seven – queen – ace.
Plan your play.
    Solution on page 52.

30. Dealer West : Both vulnerable

♠ 8 6 2
♡ A Q 8 4 2
♢ 8 7 4
♣ A 10

♠ A 3
♡ 9 7 5
♢ A 10 6 5
♣ K Q 4 2

West	North	East	South
Pass	Pass	1◇	1♠
2♡	Pass	3♡	Pass
4♡	Pass	Pass	Pass

North leads the ♠4: three – jack – six and South switches
to the ♡3: queen – king – five. North now plays the ◇2.
Plan your play.
    Solution on page 53.

27. From a National Teams Championship in 2011:

Contract: 6♡
Lead: ♠5

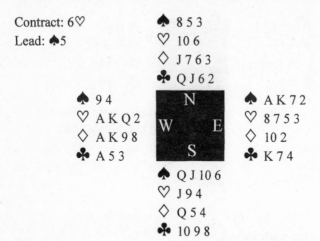

```
              ♠ 8 5 3
              ♡ 10 6
              ◇ J 7 6 3
              ♣ Q J 6 2
♠ 9 4                              ♠ A K 7 2
♡ A K Q 2         N               ♡ 8 7 5 3
◇ A K 9 8      W     E            ◇ 10 2
♣ A 5 3           S               ♣ K 7 4
              ♠ Q J 10 6
              ♡ J 9 4
              ◇ Q 5 4
              ♣ 10 9 8
```

With nine top tricks you need to score three more. After taking the spade in dummy, test the trumps. If they are 4-1, you can hope that the player with four trumps also has four diamonds and three spades, so that you can score two diamond ruffs and a spade ruff.

If trumps are 3-2, you have better chances. One option, after ♡A, ♡K, is to cash your diamond winners, ruff a diamond in dummy, come to the ♣A and ruff your other diamond loser. You hope that the player with the third trump also has four diamonds. If that works you need to ruff the third spade to reach your hand to draw the last trump and hope you are not over-ruffed. Chances are not great, and this line fails on the actual deal.

There is a better prospect, thanks to your diamond pips. Draw three rounds of trumps and take two finesses in diamonds. Cross to dummy and lead the ◇10, letting it run if South plays low. Win any return, cross to dummy again and repeat the diamond finesse. You succeed any time South has one or both diamond honours.

28. From a National Butler Trials, scored by Imps, 2011:

Contract: 5♣
Lead: ◇J

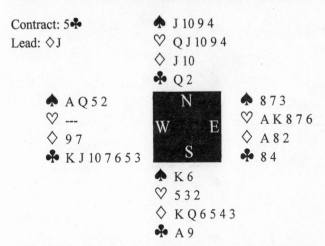

```
                    ♠ J 10 9 4
                    ♡ Q J 10 9 4
                    ◇ J 10
                    ♣ Q 2
   ♠ A Q 5 2          N          ♠ 8 7 3
   ♡ ---                         ♡ A K 8 7 6
   ◇ 9 7          W      E        ◇ A 8 2
   ♣ K J 10 7 6 5 3    S          ♣ 8 4
                    ♠ K 6
                    ♡ 5 3 2
                    ◇ K Q 6 5 4 3
                    ♣ A 9
```

You are sure to lose one spade and one club. Your task is to avoid losing more than that. After discarding a diamond and a spade on the top hearts, should you play a spade or a club? Given the 2◇ overcall at unfavourable vulnerability, it is likely that South has both the ♣A and the ♠K. If you take the spade finesse and it wins, you have to continue with the ♣K and hope the queen is singleton. It does you no good to find either opponent with the ♣A singleton. If you credit South with the ♣A, then bare ♣Q with North is not good odds. North figures not to be short in both minors.

Indeed, if North does have ♣Q singleton, you should play a trump at trick 4. South has followed to two hearts and if South began with six diamonds and ♣A-9-2, South will have at most two spades.

When you play a club, South follows with the ♣9. You must rise with the ♣K. You cannot succeed if South began with ♣A-Q-9. Normal technique is to finesse the ♣J, but this applies only if you can repeat the finesse. When the ♣K wins, play another club. Later you play ♠A and the low spade and hope the ♠K drops.

29. From a National Open Teams, 2010:

Contract: 4$\diamondsuit$ ♠ A 7 2
Lead: ♡3   ♡ K J 6 3 2
                 $\diamondsuit$ 6 3
                 ♣ A Q 7

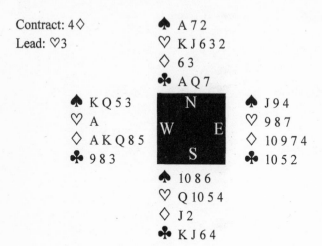

     ♠ K Q 5 3   ♠ J 9 4
     ♡ A   ♡ 9 8 7
     $\diamondsuit$ A K Q 8 5 $\diamondsuit$ 10 9 7 4
     ♣ 9 8 3   ♣ 10 5 2

                ♠ 10 8 6
                ♡ Q 10 5 4
                $\diamondsuit$ J 2
                ♣ K J 6 4

In theory you cannot make 4$\diamondsuit$ since you have one spade and three clubs to lose. You know that, but the defenders do not. You have to hope spades are 3-3, so that you can discard a club from dummy on the thirteenth spade. You could simply draw trumps and tackle the spades. That may or may not work.

You can try a little deception. The lead indicates that North's clubs are not headed by the A-K. As South has at least the ♣K and has shown up with the ♡Q, the ♠A is very likely to be with North. How about playing a low spade at trick 2? North ducks and the ♠J wins. Continue with the $\diamondsuit$4: two – queen – three and the $\diamondsuit$A. South's $\diamondsuit$J falling adds to the illusion that you are missing the $\diamondsuit$K. Now play the ♠K. If North wins and plays a club, tough luck. In practice, North took the ♠A and played a top heart, thank you.

A word about the defence. If North's ♡3 is fourth-highest or North would not bid 1♡ with K-6-3-2, South can tell West has the ♡A bare. South could play the ♡4 at trick 1 as suit-preference for clubs.

30. From National Open Teams, 2011

Contract: 4♡
Lead: ♠4

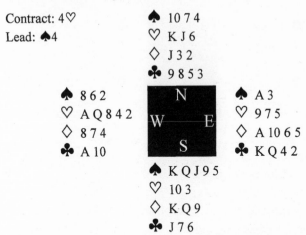

    ♠ 10 7 4
    ♡ K J 6
    ◇ J 3 2
    ♣ 9 8 5 3

♠ 8 6 2   ♠ A 3
♡ A Q 8 4 2   ♡ 9 7 5
◇ 8 7 4   ◇ A 10 6 5
♣ A 10   ♣ K Q 4 2

    ♠ K Q J 9 5
    ♡ 10 3
    ◇ K Q 9
    ♣ J 7 6

The ♠4 lead went to South, who shifted to the ♡3, queen, king. North switched to the ◇2, but it was too late. To beat 4♡ North had to lead a diamond or South had to play a diamond at trick 2.

You have lost a spade and a heart. You must hope trumps are 3-2, but even then there is sure to be a second trump loser. That means you cannot afford a diamond loser, too. Your only hope is to discard your diamond losers on the club winners in dummy and you need two discards from the clubs.

Take the ◇A and play a low club to your ten. If this loses, you will be two down, but the only realistic chance you have is to find the ♣J with South. When the ♣10 wins, cash the ♡A. All follow and you continue by cashing the ♣A, spade to the ace, ♣K, ♣Q, discarding your diamonds, diamond ruff and ruff your spade loser.

If trumps are 4-1, you will fail, but you aim for only one down via ♠A, ♣A, spade ruff and then ♣K, ♣Q. If you play the clubs before taking the spade ruff, the opponent with two trumps might ruff the fourth club and play a trump to deny you the spade ruff.

31. Dealer South : Nil vulnerable

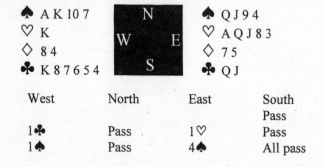

	♠ A K 4		♠ 7 6 5 2
	♡ K 6 4 3		♡ A Q 8
	♢ A 9 7 5 4		♢ Q J 10 3
	♣ 3		♣ K Q

West	North	East	South
			Pass
1♢	1♠	2♠ (1)	Pass
3♡	Pass	5♢	All pass

(1) Limit raise or stronger in diamonds

North leads the ♡J. Plan your play.
Solution on page 56.

32. Dealer South : Both vulnerable

	♠ A K 10 7		♠ Q J 9 4
	♡ K		♡ A Q J 8 3
	♢ 8 4		♢ 7 5
	♣ K 8 7 6 5 4		♣ Q J

West	North	East	South
			Pass
1♣	Pass	1♡	Pass
1♠	Pass	4♠	All pass

North leads the ♡5. Plan your play.
Solution on page 57.

33. Dealer North : North-South vulnerable

	♠ J 6 2		♠ K Q 9 3
	♡ 10 9 8 7 5		♡ A K Q
	♢ 6 5		♢ Q 7 2
	♣ A J 3		♣ K 6 2

West	North	East	South
	1♢	Double	2♠ (1)
Pass	3♢	Double	Pass
3♡	4♢	Pass	Pass
4♡	Pass	Pass	Pass

(1) 6+ spades, 0-5 points

North leads the ♢A, ♢K and a third diamond, which South ruffs with the ♡6. You over-ruff and the ♡A, ♡K draw the missing trumps. Plan your play.

Solution on page 58.

34. Dealer East : Nil vulnerable

	♠ A 7		♠ Q 9 2
	♡ K 10 9 7 2		♡ A Q J
	♢ K 5		♢ J 7 4 2
	♣ A K 9 2		♣ Q 5 4

East-West bid 1♢ : 1♡, 1NT : 2♣, 2♡ : 4♡, Pass. North leads the ♠5, thirds and fifths: queen – king – ace. You play the ♡2 to the jack and the ♢2: six – king – ace. North cashes the ♠J (♠4 from South) followed by the ♠6: nine – ten – ♡7. You continue with the ♢5: nine – four – ten from South, who returns a trump to dummy's queen, North following. You try the ♢7, hoping to drop the ♢Q. South plays the ♢8, you ruff and North plays the ♢3. You have had no luck so far. How will you conclude the play?

Solution on page 59.

31. From the 2011 Asia-Pacific Teams:

Contract: 5♦
Lead: ♡J

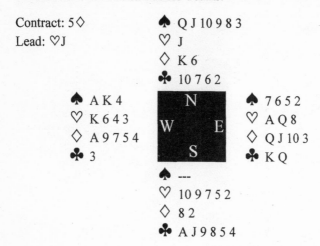

                  ♠ Q J 10 9 8 3
                  ♡ J
                  ♦ K 6
                  ♣ 10 7 6 2

♠ A K 4   ♠ 7 6 5 2
♡ K 6 4 3   ♡ A Q 8
♦ A 9 7 5 4   ♦ Q J 10 3
♣ 3   ♣ K Q

                  ♠ ---
                  ♡ 10 9 7 5 2
                  ♦ 8 2
                  ♣ A J 9 8 5 4

East-West did well to avoid 3NT. It will make ten tricks on a spade lead, but is two down on a club lead.

When the contract looks comfortable, it is easy to take your eye off the ball. You have a club loser, but the second club will take care of the spade loser. You can make 11 tricks or, if the ♦K is onside, 12 tricks. Declarer did not foresee the danger when he won with the ♡A and took the diamond finesse. North won and shifted to a club. South won and returned the ♡10. North ruffed and the spade return, ruffed by South, took the contract two down.

When everything looks rosy, ask yourself, 'What could go wrong?' Your task is to make 11 tricks. You should not jeopardize your contract for a possible overtrick. On the bidding the ♦K is likely to be with North anyway. Win the heart lead and play ♦A and another diamond. You lose only to the ♦K and the ♣A.

Many were in 6♦ failing and in 5♦ one off after the spade lead. The only declarer in 5♦ on the heart lead took the diamond finesse and was two off.

32. From the 2011 Asia-Pacific Teams:

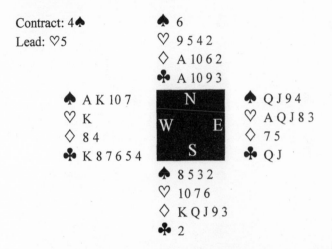

Contract: 4♠
Lead: ♡5

♠ 6
♡ 9 5 4 2
♢ A 10 6 2
♣ A 10 9 3

♠ A K 10 7
♡ K
♢ 8 4
♣ K 8 7 6 5 4

♠ Q J 9 4
♡ A Q J 8 3
♢ 7 5
♣ Q J

♠ 8 5 3 2
♡ 10 7 6
♢ K Q J 9 3
♣ 2

North could have beaten 4♠ with a diamond lead or ♣A and
another club, but neither of those starts was attractive. North
chose the ♡5, second highest from three or four rags.

There are several lines that will allow 4♠ to succeed, but not the
one actually chosen by West, who won the opening lead with the
♡K. He played ♠A, ♠K and then led a low club. North won and
tried the ♢A. South discouraged with the ♢Q and so North
played a club. South ruffed and cashed a diamond for one down.

West was hoping for a normal break in clubs, but one would think
it is more urgent to pitch one or both diamond losers on the hearts.
You could win trick 1 with the ♡A and immediately play ♡Q,
♡J. As long as you remove one diamond loser, all should be well.
Another option, and a sensible one, is to win trick 1 with the ♡K
and play ♠A and a spade to the queen. Then discard a diamond
on a winning heart. If you judge it safe, play another heart. If not,
play a diamond and plan to ruff a diamond later.

33. From the 2011 European Open Teams:

Contract: 4♡
Lead: ◇A, ◇K and
a third diamond

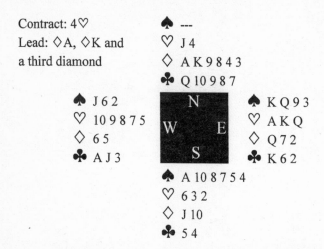

```
                    ♠ ---
                    ♡ J 4
                    ◇ A K 9 8 4 3
                    ♣ Q 10 9 8 7
    ♠ J 6 2              N              ♠ K Q 9 3
    ♡ 10 9 8 7 5                        ♡ A K Q
    ◇ 6 5          W         E          ◇ Q 7 2
    ♣ A J 3              S              ♣ K 6 2
                    ♠ A 10 8 7 5 4
                    ♡ 6 3 2
                    ◇ J 10
                    ♣ 5 4
```

It would have been attractive to double 4◇, but it is too late to
worry about that. South showed six spades in the bidding and has
turned up with two diamonds and three hearts. Hence South has
only two clubs and so North has five clubs. Therefore the ♣Q is
very likely to be with North. The location of the ♣Q makes no
difference to you, as you do not plan to take the club finesse. You
plan to endplay either North or South, according to their choice.

Since South is down to six spades and two clubs, you play the
♣K and ♣A, followed by a low spade to the king. With only
spades left, if South takes the ♠A, he has to return a spade to give
you an extra trick there. If South ducks, you play a low spade from
dummy and again South must duck. When your ♠J wins, you exit
with your club loser. North wins, but whether he plays back a
diamond or a club, you ruff in dummy and discard your spade loser.

Playing the deal in exactly this fashion to make 4♡ was Vytautas
Vainikonis of Lithuania.

34. From the World Team Championships, 2011

Contract: 4♡
Lead: ♠5

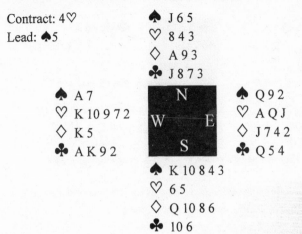

```
                        ♠ J 6 5
                        ♡ 8 4 3
                        ◇ A 9 3
                        ♣ J 8 7 3
    ♠ A 7                                    ♠ Q 9 2
    ♡ K 10 9 7 2              N              ♡ A Q J
    ◇ K 5             W              E       ◇ J 7 4 2
    ♣ A K 9 2                 S              ♣ Q 5 4
                        ♠ K 10 8 4 3
                        ♡ 6 5
                        ◇ Q 10 8 6
                        ♣ 10 6
```

1. ♠5: queen – king – ace   2. ♡2: three – jack – five
3. ◇2: six – king – ace   4. ♠J: two – four – seven
5. ♠6: nine – ten – ♡7
6. ◇5: nine – four – ten (you figured North would rise with ◇Q)
7. ♡6: nine – four – queen   8. ◇7: eight – ♡10 – ◇3

You have the ♡K and four clubs, dummy has ♡A, ◇J and three
clubs. Anything works if clubs are 3-3. If not, you have to choose
between four clubs with the last trump (play three rounds of
clubs, ruff the fourth) or four clubs with the ◇Q (play a trump to
squeeze that hand). To decide, go back to the opening lead.

North led the ♠5 and turned up with ♠J, ♠6. South has shown
up with ♠K, ♠10. North cannot have the ♠8. That would make
the ♠5 fourth highest. North might have three or four spades, not
five. Therefore South must have at least four spades. The diamond
play marks South with the queen, but South cannot be squeezed.
South cannot have four spades, two hearts (known), four diamonds
and four clubs. A world champion declarer in fact played to the
♡A and went down. He should have played to ruff a club.

35. Dealer West : North-South vulnerable

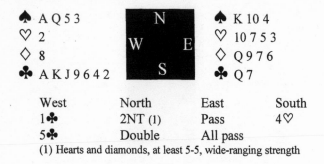

♠ A Q 5 3   ♠ K 10 4
♡ 2   ♡ 10 7 5 3
◇ 8   ◇ Q 9 7 6
♣ A K J 9 6 4 2   ♣ Q 7

West	North	East	South
1♣	2NT (1)	Pass	4♡
5♣	Double	All pass	

(1) Hearts and diamonds, at least 5-5, wide-ranging strength

North leads the ♡A, followed by the ♡6 to South's queen, which you ruff. Plan your play.

Solution on page 62.

36. Dealer South : East-West vulnerable

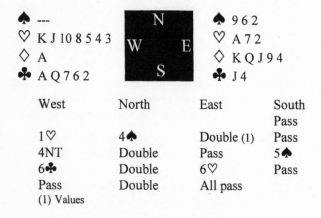

♠ ---   ♠ 9 6 2
♡ K J 10 8 5 4 3   ♡ A 7 2
◇ A   ◇ K Q J 9 4
♣ A Q 7 6 2   ♣ J 4

West	North	East	South
			Pass
1♡	4♠	Double (1)	Pass
4NT	Double	Pass	5♠
6♣	Double	6♡	Pass
Pass	Double	All pass	

(1) Values

North leads the ♠A. Plan your play.

Solution on page 63.

37. Dealer South : East-West vulnerable

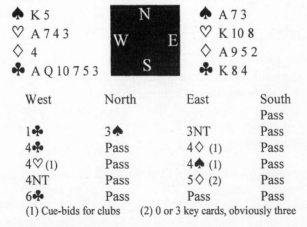

♠ K Q 10 6 4 2
♡ J 6 3
◇ K 5 3
♣ K

♠ 9 8 5 3
♡ A 9 2
◇ 9
♣ A 8 6 5 2

West	North	East	South
			Pass
1♠	Pass	2NT (1)	Pass
4♠	Pass	Pass	Pass

(1) Spade raise

North leads the ◇Q: nine – ace – five and South returns the
♡4: six – queen . . . Plan your play.
Solution on page 64.

38. Dealer South : Nil vulnerable

♠ K 5
♡ A 7 4 3
◇ 4
♣ A Q 10 7 5 3

♠ A 7 3
♡ K 10 8
◇ A 9 5 2
♣ K 8 4

West	North	East	South
			Pass
1♣	3♠	3NT	Pass
4♣	Pass	4◇ (1)	Pass
4♡ (1)	Pass	4♠ (1)	Pass
4NT	Pass	5◇ (2)	Pass
6♣	Pass	Pass	Pass

(1) Cue-bids for clubs   (2) 0 or 3 key cards, obviously three

North leads the ♠Q: three – six – king. You play the ♣A: jack –
four – two. Plan your play.
Solution on page 65.

35. From the 2011 World Team Championships:

Contract: 5♣ doubled
Lead: ♡A

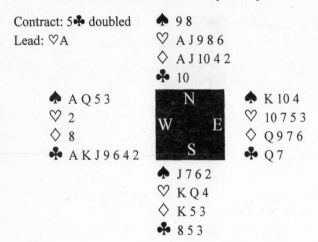

♠ 9 8
♡ A J 9 8 6
♢ A J 10 4 2
♣ 10

♠ A Q 5 3
♡ 2
♢ 8
♣ A K J 9 6 4 2

♠ K 10 4
♡ 10 7 5 3
♢ Q 9 7 6
♣ Q 7

♠ J 7 6 2
♡ K Q 4
♢ K 5 3
♣ 8 5 3

You have bought a very suitable dummy. You have no club losers, but you are sure to lose two tricks in the red suits. You have to avoid losing a spade, if possible. North is known to be at least 5-5 in the red suits, but spades might be 3-3. North could be 3-5-5-0.

That is not a strong chance, but North could have the ♠J singleton or doubleton. That would also give you four spade tricks. The other chances are when North has two spades in a 2-5-5-1 pattern or North might be 1-1 in the black suits or have no clubs with one or two spades (although with the more extreme shapes, North might have preferred to bid 5♡).

Your basic plan should be to play a club to the queen and then start on the spades. That will be fine if spades are 3-3 or the ♠J comes down short or in the actual layout above. After ♣Q and three rounds of spades you can ruff the fourth spade in comfort. If it turns out that North began with a singleton low spade and two clubs, then you were not going to make 5♣ anyway.

36. From a National Open Teams, 2011:

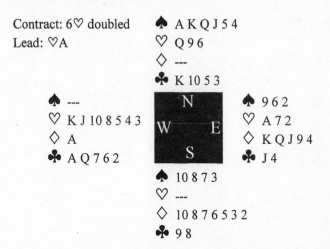

Contract: 6♡ doubled
Lead: ♡A

North:
♠ A K Q J 5 4
♡ Q 9 6
◇ ---
♣ K 10 5 3

West:
♠ ---
♡ K J 10 8 5 4 3
◇ A
♣ A Q 7 6 2

East:
♠ 9 6 2
♡ A 7 2
◇ K Q J 9 4
♣ J 4

South:
♠ 10 8 7 3
♡ ---
◇ 10 8 7 6 5 3 2
♣ 9 8

There are clearly no problems if the hearts divide 2-1. You lose at most one club. If the trumps are 3-0, which opponent is likely to have the three? North has pre-empted with 4♠, but that was opposite a passed partner and after an opposition opening bid and so North can have a decent hand. Indeed, North's double of 4NT indicates that North does have a strong hand. Would South have run to 5♠ if holding ♡Q-9-6? That seems doubtful. North's double of 6♣ implies the ♣K. Would North have doubled 6♡ with no more than powerful spades and the ♣K?

The evidence is strong that North has the ♡Q and so Magnus Magnusson (Iceland) played the ♡A at trick 2. What next?

He backed his judgment that North had the ♣K, too. After drawing trumps, West cashed the ◇A and led a low club for twelve tricks and +1660. Note that if West plays the ◇A before drawing trumps, North ruffs and West still has to lose a club.

37. From the 2011 European Mixed Teams:

Contract: 4♠
Lead: ◇Q

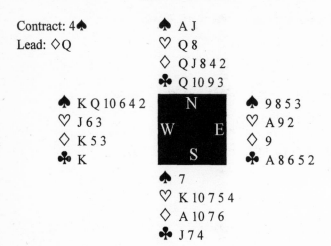

                    ♠ A J
                    ♡ Q 8
                    ◇ Q J 8 4 2
                    ♣ Q 10 9 3

♠ K Q 10 6 4 2   ♠ 9 8 5 3
♡ J 6 3   ♡ A 9 2
◇ K 5 3   ◇ 9
♣ K   ♣ A 8 6 5 2

                    ♠ 7
                    ♡ K 10 7 5 4
                    ◇ A 10 7 6
                    ♣ J 7 4

North led the ◇Q against 4♠. South took the ◇A and switched to the ♡4, low from West, queen from North. Declarer took the ♡A, crossed to the ♣K and discarded a heart from dummy on the ◇K. Next came the ♠K. North won, played the ♡8 to South's ♡K and the third heart enabled North to score the ♠J for one down.

West should duck North's ♡Q and win the heart return with the ace. No other return by North troubles West. Then play ♣K, ◇K, discarding a heart from dummy, and the ♠K. As North cannot reach the South hand any more, declarer has no further problems. Successful options exist after taking the ♡A at trick 2, such as ♣K, ◇K, ◇5, discarding both hearts from dummy or ♣K, ◇K, diamond ruff, ♣A and another club, pitching both of West's hearts.

Is there a risk of a heart ruff? If the ♡Q is singleton, South has six hearts to the K-10 and the ◇A, enough for a weak two opening. South would certainly not have the ♠A as well. If South's ♡4 is singleton, North would have played the ♡10, not the ♡Q. Since a heart has to be lost anyway, ducking at trick 2 will not cost.

38. From the 2011 White House Junior International:

Contract: 6♣
Lead: ♠Q

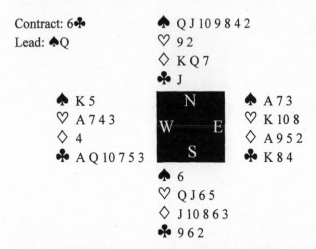

```
              ♠ Q J 10 9 8 4 2
              ♡ 9 2
              ◊ K Q 7
              ♣ J
♠ K 5                            ♠ A 7 3
♡ A 7 4 3        N               ♡ K 10 8
◊ 4           W     E            ◊ A 9 5 2
♣ A Q 10 7 5 3   S               ♣ K 8 4
              ♠ 6
              ♡ Q J 6 5
              ◊ J 10 8 6 3
              ♣ 9 6 2
```

There are a number of ways to succeed, but after the spade lead, taken by the king, and the ♣A, on which North dropped the jack, Lotan Fisher, en route to Israel's winning the event, produced a simple and successful line. At trick 3 he played a low heart to dummy's ten. South won and exited with a diamond.

Declarer took the ◊A and played a club to the queen to confirm the trump layout. As North would not have a 7-4-1-1 pattern with four hearts (that would give South seven good diamonds and South had passed as dealer), it was perfectly safe for West to continue with the ♡K and ♡A. When the hearts were not 3-3, West ruffed his heart loser in dummy.

He returned to hand with a diamond ruff and drew the missing trump. That was worth 10 Imps as the contract at the other table was 3NT, which made twelve tricks. It is worth noting how an opposition pre-empt so often helps declarer in planning the play.

39. Dealer South : Both vulnerable

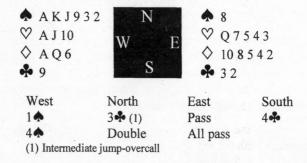

	♠ J 7 5 2		♠ 4
	♡ ---		♡ J 10 8 6 2
	◇ K J 9 6 3 2		◇ A 10 8
	♣ A 7 6		♣ K J 4 3

West	North	East	South
			1♡
2◇	2♠	3♠ (1)	Pass
4◇	4♠	5◇	Double
Pass	Pass	Pass	

(1) Strong diamond raise

North leads the ♠A, ♠8 from South, and continues with the ♠Q, which you ruff with the ◇8. South over-ruffs with the ◇Q and switches to the ♡A. You ruff with the ◇2 and North follows with the ♡7. Plan your play.

Solution on page 68.

40. Dealer West : East-West vulnerable

	♠ A K J 9 3 2		♠ 8
	♡ A J 10		♡ Q 7 5 4 3
	◇ A Q 6		◇ 10 8 5 4 2
	♣ 9		♣ 3 2

West	North	East	South
1♠	3♣ (1)	Pass	4♣
4♠	Double	All pass	

(1) Intermediate jump-overcall

North leads the ♣A, followed by the ♣10: two – queen – ♠2. Plan your play.

Solution on page 69.

41. Dealer West : East-West vulnerable

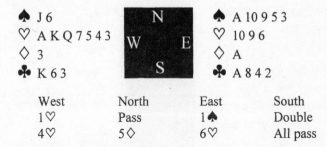

♠ J 6
♥ A K Q 7 5 4 3
♦ 3
♣ K 6 3

♠ A 10 9 5 3
♥ 10 9 6
♦ A
♣ A 8 4 2

West	North	East	South
1♥	Pass	1♠	Double
4♥	5◇	6♥	All pass

North leads the ♣9: two – seven – king. When you play the ♥A, South discards the ◇2. Plan your play.

Solution on page 70.

42. Dealer North : North-South vulnerable

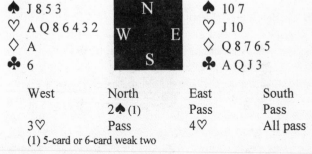

♠ J 8 5 3
♥ A Q 8 6 4 3 2
♦ A
♣ 6

♠ 10 7
♥ J 10
♦ Q 8 7 6 5
♣ A Q J 3

West	North	East	South
	2♠ (1)	Pass	Pass
3♥	Pass	4♥	All pass

(1) 5-card or 6-card weak two

North leads the ♠A, ♠K. South follows with the ♠9, ♠6. West continues with the ♠4. Plan the play?

Solution on page 71.

39. From the final of a National Open Teams, 2011:

Contract: 5◇ doubled
Lead: ♠A

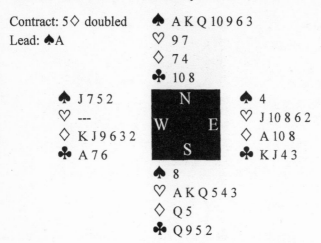

The ♠Q came next, ruffed with the ◇8. South over-ruffed and switched to the ♡A. West ruffed low, ruffed a spade, crossed to the ♣A and ruffed his last spade. He ruffed a heart low, drew trumps and finessed the ♣J. When that lost, he was one down.

After trick 2, the first thing to note is that North began with seven spades. South should have returned a trump at trick 3 to beat you. North would have switched to a heart if holding a singleton. You should also deduce that North has at least two hearts (South would have bid 4♡ with seven to the A-K-Q). Therefore after heart ruff, spade ruff, you should ruff a heart low, ruff your last spade and ruff a third heart high. You can then draw trumps and when North follows twice, you know North began with a 7-2-2-2 pattern.

Continue with the diamonds, discarding a heart and two clubs from dummy. You are left with ♣A-7-6 and dummy has ♡J and ♣K-J. Holding on to the ♡Q, South must come down to two clubs and after ♣K, ♣A, your last club is high. The chance of the ♣Q with South is far greater than South having all four diamonds.

40. From a 2010 match between Australia and New Zealand:

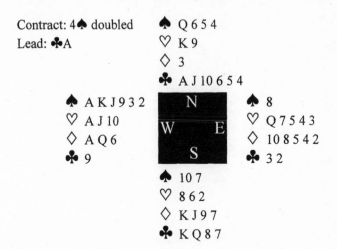

Contract: 4♠ doubled
Lead: ♣A

```
                    ♠ Q 6 5 4
                    ♡ K 9
                    ◇ 3
                    ♣ A J 10 6 5 4
   ♠ A K J 9 3 2                    ♠ 8
   ♡ A J 10          N              ♡ Q 7 5 4 3
   ◇ A Q 6      W         E         ◇ 10 8 5 4 2
   ♣ 9               S              ♣ 3 2
                    ♠ 10 7
                    ♡ 8 6 2
                    ◇ K J 9 7
                    ♣ K Q 8 7
```

West ruffed the club continuation and played ♠A, ♠K, ♠J. North won and persisted with a club, forcing West to ruff. West drew North's last trump, but was out of trumps himself. He played ♡A and another heart, but North won and cashed the rest of the clubs. West made the ◇A, but that was only seven tricks and –800.

With six trumps missing, the normal break is 4-2 and, given North's double, it was not hard to predict that spades would not be 3-3. In these situations one can sometimes survive by leaving a trump in dummy to take care of the next ruff and to set up a side suit before starting on the trumps. That would work on the actual layout.

West ruffs the second club and plays the ♡J. North wins, but what can North do? West would win a heart return with the ace and play ♠A, ♠K, ♠J. If North plays a third club after taking the ♡K, dummy ruffs and West discards a diamond. Then West is in control after ♠A, ♠K, ♠J. North wins, but West can ruff the next club, draw the last trump and use dummy's hearts to discard the other diamond loser.

41. From the semi-finals of a National Open Teams, 2011:

Contract: 6♡
Lead: ♣9

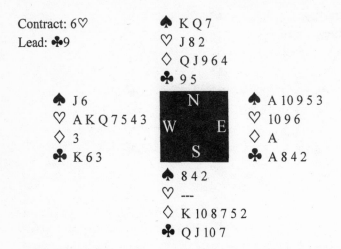

♠ K Q 7
♡ J 8 2
◇ Q J 9 6 4
♣ 9 5

♠ J 6
♡ A K Q 7 5 4 3
◇ 3
♣ K 6 3

♠ A 10 9 5 3
♡ 10 9 6
◇ A
♣ A 8 4 2

♠ 8 4 2
♡ ---
◇ K 10 8 7 5 2
♣ Q J 10 7

North led the ♣9 against 6♡. Declarer won in hand and drew trumps. He then played the ♠6: seven – ace – two and the ♠3: four – jack – king. West took the club return with the ace and led the ♠10: eight – ♣6 – ♠Q. One down.

For a player of international standard, this was a very weak line. He let himself be fooled by North's ♠K. No doubt West felt that South would have some values in spades to justify the takeout double. Persuaded by the vulnerability South had doubled on the good shape, not on high card strength.

There is nothing wrong with playing South for one or both spade honours, but it costs nothing for West to lead the ♠J after drawing trumps. This will always work if North has ♠K-x or ♠Q-x, which is the situation for which West played, or if the actual position exists. If the ♠J loses to South and the ♠A does not fetch the other honour and South plays low on the ♠10 on the third round of spades, then and only then will West need to divine the position.

42. From the 2010 World Senior Teams:

Contract: 4♡
Lead: ♠A, then ♠K
and a low spade

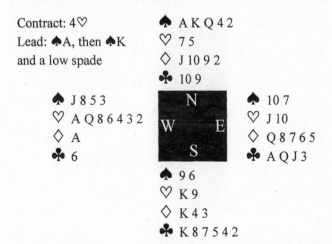

```
              ♠ A K Q 4 2
              ♡ 7 5
              ◇ J 10 9 2
              ♣ 10 9
  ♠ J 8 5 3          N          ♠ 10 7
  ♡ A Q 8 6 4 3 2  W   E        ♡ J 10
  ◇ A                 S         ◇ Q 8 7 6 5
  ♣ 6                           ♣ A Q J 3
              ♠ 9 6
              ♡ K 9
              ◇ K 4 3
              ♣ K 8 7 5 4 2
```

As North is known to have started with five spades to the A-K-Q, South is marked with the missing kings. The natural inclination is to ruff trick 3 in dummy. If you do that, South will over-ruff and return a trump. You will be left with a spade loser at the end.

Liz McGowan of Scotland found the solution. She simply discarded a diamond on the third spade. South ruffed and returned a diamond. West won and cashed the ♡A. When the ♡K dropped West simply ruffed her remaining spade loser and had ten tricks.

Discarding from dummy at trick 3 is just as effective if South began with the ♡K singleton. There was no successful move if South had started with ♡K-x-x or ♡K-x-x-x.

43. Dealer West : North-South vulnerable

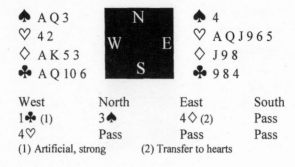

♠ A Q 3
♡ 4 2
◇ A K 5 3
♣ A Q 10 6

♠ 4
♡ A Q J 9 6 5
◇ J 9 8
♣ 9 8 4

West	North	East	South
1♣ (1)	3♠	4◇ (2)	Pass
4♡	Pass	Pass	Pass
(1) Artificial, strong		(2) Transfer to hearts	

North leads the ♣5: four – jack – queen. Plan your play.
Solution on page 74.

44. Dealer West : Nil vulnerable

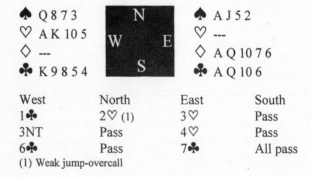

♠ Q 8 7 3
♡ A K 10 5
◇ ---
♣ K 9 8 5 4

♠ A J 5 2
♡ ---
◇ A Q 10 7 6
♣ A Q 10 6

West	North	East	South
1♣	2♡ (1)	3♡	Pass
3NT	Pass	4♡	Pass
6♣	Pass	7♣	All pass
(1) Weak jump-overcall			

Perhaps East and West were both a bit pushy, but that is not your
concern. North leads the ♣2: six – jack – king. Plan your play.
Solution on page 75.

Test your play

73

45. Dealer South : Nil vulnerable

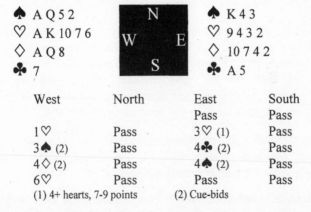

	♠ A K 9 6		♠ Q 7 2
	♡ K		♡ A Q 10 4 2
	◇ 8 6		◇ 9 5 3
	♣ Q J 8 7 5 2		♣ 10 4

West	North	East	South
			1◇
2♣	Pass	2♡	Pass
2♠	Pass	3♣	All pass

North leads the ♡7: two – three – king. You play a low spade to
the queen and cash ♡A, ♡Q, discarding your diamonds. All
follow, but the ♡J has not appeared. How would you continue?
Solution on page 76.

46. Dealer East : North-South vulnerable

	♠ A Q 5 2		♠ K 4 3
	♡ A K 10 7 6		♡ 9 4 3 2
	◇ A Q 8		◇ 10 7 4 2
	♣ 7		♣ A 5

West	North	East	South
		Pass	Pass
1♡	Pass	3♡ (1)	Pass
3♠ (2)	Pass	4♣ (2)	Pass
4◇ (2)	Pass	4♠ (2)	Pass
6♡	Pass	Pass	Pass
(1) 4+ hearts, 7-9 points		(2) Cue-bids	

North leads the ♣K. Plan your play. How would you manage the
play if trumps are (a) 2-2? (b) 3-1 and you have a trump loser?
Solution on page 77.

43. Board 50 from the semi-finals of the 2011 Bermuda Bowl:

Contract: 4♡
Lead: ♣5

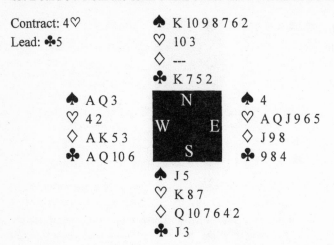

```
              ♠ K 10 9 8 7 6 2
              ♡ 10 3
              ◇ ---
              ♣ K 7 5 2
♠ A Q 3                          ♠ 4
♡ 4 2                            ♡ A Q J 9 6 5
◇ A K 5 3                        ◇ J 9 8
♣ A Q 10 6                       ♣ 9 8 4
              ♠ J 5
              ♡ K 8 7
              ◇ Q 10 7 6 4 2
              ♣ J 3
```

The contract was 4♡ at all four tables. One West declarer and one East received a spade lead and made eleven tricks. At the other two tables West was declarer and North led a low club.

Given the 3♠ pre-empt, the ♡K is likely to be with South and the club lead might easily be a singleton. That indicates a heart to the ace at trick 2, followed by the ♡Q. That should guarantee the contract. With the ♣J gone, you can set up a club winner to discard a diamond loser from dummy. As the cards lie, after ♡A, ♡Q, West should have no trouble making eleven tricks.

After the club lead both declarers finessed the ♡Q at trick 2. One South won and returned the ◇4, ace, ruffed. North played a spade. West won, drew trumps and lost a trick to the ♣K, +420.

The other South took the ♡K and returned the ♣3. West can survive by playing the ♣A and drawing trumps, but West played low. North won and gave South a club ruff. South switched to a low diamond, ace, ruffed. When North led another club, West was two down. How much easier to play ♡A, ♡Q at tricks 2 and 3!

44. From the 2011 World Transnational Open Teams:

Contract: 7♣
Lead: ♣2

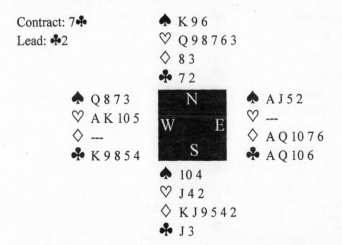

♠ K 9 6
♡ Q 9 8 7 6 3
♢ 8 3
♣ 7 2

♠ Q 8 7 3
♡ A K 10 5
♢ ---
♣ K 9 8 5 4

♠ A J 5 2
♡ ---
♢ A Q 10 7 6
♣ A Q 10 6

♠ 10 4
♡ J 4 2
♢ K J 9 5 4 2
♣ J 3

It is vital to eliminate, as far as possible, any emotional reaction to the sight of dummy. Emotion can cloud your thought processes, whether the emotion is euphoria or despondency. No doubt West was displeased with East's bidding, since the contract seemed to depend on the spade finesse. Given the weak jump-overcall by North, the ♠K was likely to be offside. West embarked on a no-play line and went one down.

With a clear head, West would normally have made the grand slam. After capturing South's ♣J, play ♡A, ♡K and discard two spades from dummy. Then finesse the ♠J. When that wins there are several ways to continue. You can draw trumps, cash the ♠A, discard a heart on the ♢A, ruff a diamond, ruff a spade, ruff a diamond and claim.

If it turns out that the ♠K is with South, you and partner can discuss the auction after the session has ended. Arguments at the table are definitely counter-productive.

45. From the final of the 2010 NEC Cup:

Contract: 3♣
Lead: ♡7

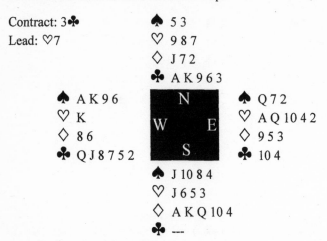

```
                    ♠ 5 3
                    ♡ 9 8 7
                    ◇ J 7 2
                    ♣ A K 9 6 3
    ♠ A K 9 6          N          ♠ Q 7 2
    ♡ K                           ♡ A Q 10 4 2
    ◇ 8 6         W       E       ◇ 9 5 3
    ♣ Q J 8 7 5 2        S        ♣ 10 4
                    ♠ J 10 8 4
                    ♡ J 6 5 3
                    ◇ A K Q 10 4
                    ♣ ---
```

The defence can always defeat 3♣, either by starting with ♣A, ♣K and switching to diamonds or by leading a diamond. South continues diamonds. West ruffs the third round, but North can make sure of scoring three club tricks.

The heart lead was a bonanza for West, who won, crossed to the ♠Q and ditched his diamonds on ♡A, ♡Q. At this point you can play almost any card and succeed. The easiest is to plan to ruff your fourth spade. Either play ♠A, ♠K at once or ruff a diamond and then lead a club or play ♠A, ♠K. What can North do? If he ruffs the third spade and cashes ♣A, ♣K to prevent the spade ruff, you lose three clubs and a spade. If not, you have it just as easy.

In practice, after trick 4, West played the only card from dummy to allow the defence to prevail. He played the ♣4 to the queen and king. North cashed the ♣A and switched to diamonds. West ruffed and was down to ♠A-K-9 and ♣J-8-7. He had lost two tricks and could not prevent the defence from scoring a spade and two more trump tricks.

46. From the quarter-finals, 2010 NEC Cup:

Contract: 6♡
Lead: ♣K

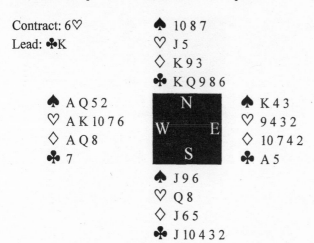

```
                    ♠ 10 8 7
                    ♡ J 5
                    ◇ K 9 3
                    ♣ K Q 9 8 6
♠ A Q 5 2                        ♠ K 4 3
♡ A K 10 7 6          N          ♡ 9 4 3 2
◇ A Q 8          W       E       ◇ 10 7 4 2
♣ 7                  S          ♣ A 5
                    ♠ J 9 6
                    ♡ Q 8
                    ◇ J 6 5
                    ♣ J 10 4 3 2
```

The slam is not marvellous and would be likely to fail if you have a trump loser. Once you are in 6♡ you must make the most of your good fortune. You should recognize that the diamond combination offers the chance of an endplay. Therefore take the ♣A and ruff the ♣5 at once.

(a) When you cash ♡A, ♡K and find trumps 2-2, play ♠K, ♠A, ♠Q. Whether they are 3-3 or not, ruff the last spade in dummy and lead a low diamond. If South follows low, play the ◇8. North can win, but must lead a diamond into your A-Q or give you a ruff-and-discard. If South plays the ◇9 or ◇J on the first diamond, play the ◇Q to ensure the slam. Take no credit if you finessed the ◇Q, although South did have the ◇K on the actual deal.

(b) After the club ruff and ♡A, ♡K, if you have a trump loser, cross to the ♠K and finesse the ◇Q. When that wins (else you are down), cash the ◇A, ♠A, ♠Q and hope spades are 3-3. Then exit with a trump. If the opponent with the last trump has only clubs left, the forced ruff-and-discard allows you to succeed.

47. Dealer North : East-West vulnerable

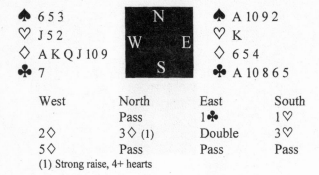

♠ 6 5 3
♡ J 5 2
◇ A K Q J 10 9
♣ 7

♠ A 10 9 2
♡ K
◇ 6 5 4
♣ A 10 8 6 5

West	North	East	South
	Pass	1♣	1♡
2◇	3◇ (1)	Double	3♡
5◇	Pass	Pass	Pass

(1) Strong raise, 4+ hearts

North leads the ♡3: king – ace – five. South switches to the ◇8.
Plan your play.

Solution on page 80.

48. Dealer South : North-South vulnerable

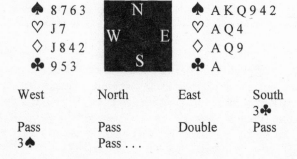

♠ 8 7 6 3
♡ J 7
◇ J 8 4 2
♣ 9 5 3

♠ A K Q 9 4 2
♡ A Q 4
◇ A Q 9
♣ A

West	North	East	South
			3♣
Pass	Pass	Double	Pass
3♠	Pass ...		

East continues with 4NT and 5NT and, finding West with no
kings, signs off in 6♠. North leads the ♣6. When you play the
♠A, ♠K, ♠Q, North discards a diamond and two hearts.
Plan your play.

Solution on page 81.

49. Dealer North : Nil vulnerable

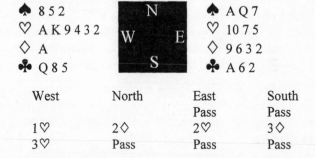

♠ 8
♡ 10 8 6 5
◇ K 4
♣ K 9 8 7 5 2

♠ A Q 10 9 5 3
♡ A 4 3
◇ 6
♣ A J 6

West	North	East	South
	Pass	1♠	3◇ (1)
Double	Pass	4◇	Pass
5♣	Pass	6♣	All pass

(1) Pre-emptive

North leads the ◇3: six – ace – four and South returns the ◇Q: king – eight – ♡3. Plan your play.

Solution on page 82.

50. Dealer East : Both vulnerable

♠ 8 5 2
♡ A K 9 4 3 2
◇ A
♣ Q 8 5

♠ A Q 7
♡ 10 7 5
◇ 9 6 3 2
♣ A 6 2

West	North	East	South
		Pass	Pass
1♡	2◇	2♡	3◇
3♡	Pass	Pass	Pass

North leads the ◇K. You play ♡A, ♡K and South discards the ♠3, low-encouraging, on the second heart. Defenders do not always signal genuinely and so you play the ♠5: six – queen – king. South returns the ◇10, which you ruff. Plan your play.

Solution on page 83.

47. From the 2011 World Transnational Open Teams:

Contract: 5◇
Lead: ♡3

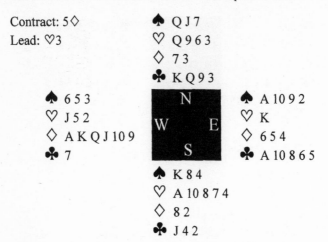

♠ Q J 7
♡ Q 9 6 3
◇ 7 3
♣ K Q 9 3

♠ 6 5 3
♡ J 5 2
◇ A K Q J 10 9
♣ 7

♠ A 10 9 2
♡ K
◇ 6 5 4
♣ A 10 8 6 5

♠ K 8 4
♡ A 10 8 7 4
◇ 8 2
♣ J 4 2

There are a number of ways to defeat 5◇, but a heart lead to the ace and a trump switch is not one of those ways. Declarer took the trump switch and played ♣A, club ruff, heart ruff, club ruff, heart ruff, club ruff. This set up dummy's last club as a winner. West drew the missing trumps, crossed to the ♠A and cashed the club winner. He made six diamonds in hand, two in dummy, two clubs and a spade for +600. At the other table West was in 3NT on a heart lead and the defence took the first five tricks.

In 5◇, after heart lead, trump switch, it is vital to start on the clubs before ruffing a heart. If you ruff a heart first, you are an entry short to establish the clubs and reach dummy to cash the fifth club.

Any lead by North can defeat 5◇. A trump lead will do it easily enough, particularly if South plays a second trump when in with the ♡A. After a heart lead, king, ace, South can beat 5◇ by switching to a spade to knock out the late entry to the established club winner or by returning a heart. That takes out one of dummy's entries before declarer has started on the club ruffs.

48. From a 2010 National Swiss Pairs, scored by Imps:

Contract: 6♠
Lead: ♣6

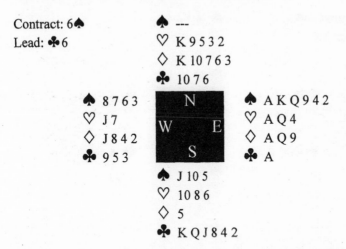

```
                  ♠ ---
                  ♡ K 9 5 3 2
                  ◇ K 10 7 6 3
                  ♣ 10 7 6
  ♠ 8 7 6 3            N          ♠ A K Q 9 4 2
  ♡ J 7          W         E      ♡ A Q 4
  ◇ J 8 4 2                       ◇ A Q 9
  ♣ 9 5 3            S            ♣ A
                  ♠ J 10 5
                  ♡ 10 8 6
                  ◇ 5
                  ♣ K Q J 8 4 2
```

As West might have had no values at all, East took some risk, pushing to slam. On the other hand, nothing ventured, nothing gained. West might also have had two kings. Chances are good that West would have one king.

At the table West played the ◇Q at trick 5 and North grabbed the ◇K. North exited with a club, ruffed in dummy. West had it easy from there and cashed the ◇A, ◇J, followed by the heart finesse for twelve tricks. North would have done better to duck the ◇K. Now the defence can succeed, no matter how West proceeds.

Given South's 3♣ opening and North's void in spades, North is sure to have length in both red suits. It is also very likely that North has both red kings. After drawing trumps the winning move, as the cards lie, is to play the ♡Q. If North ducks this, West loses only to the ◇K. If North takes the ♡Q, West has two entries, the ♡J and ruffing the ♡A. West can then lead the ◇J, king, ace, and return to hand to finesse against the ◇10.

49. From the final of the 2009 World Senior Teams:

Contract: 6♣   ♠ K J 6 4
Lead: ◇3   ♡ Q 9 7
                    ◇ 10 8 3
                    ♣ Q 10 4

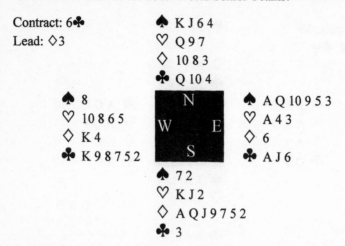

        ♠ 8   ♠ A Q 10 9 5 3
        ♡ 10 8 6 5   ♡ A 4 3
        ◇ K 4   ◇ 6
        ♣ K 9 8 7 5 2   ♣ A J 6

                    ♠ 7 2
                    ♡ K J 2
                    ◇ A Q J 9 7 5 2
                    ♣ 3

In the Open final, the USA was –50 in 3◇ North-South and –50 in 6♣ East-West. In the Women's final, the USA was –100 in 3♡ East-West and China was –50 in 4♠ East-West. The only place where contracts actually made was in the Senior Teams final.

Poland played in 5♣, England in 6♣. Both Norths led a diamond to the ace and both Souths returned a diamond to the king. Since you cannot eliminate dummy's remaining heart loser, you have to establish dummy's spades to discard your heart losers. The English West played a spade to the queen and ruffed a low spade. Since South had pre-empted with 3◇, declarer placed the ♣Q with North. He played a low club to the jack and ruffed another low spade. Then came ♣K, club to the ace and dummy's three spade winners allowed West to discard his heart losers.

After the first spade ruff, West might have played more safely via ♣K and then a finesse of the ♣J. That is how the Polish declarer played and also made twelve tricks. The first-round club finesse risked losing to the singleton ♣Q.

50. From a National Pairs in 2010:

Contract: 3♡
Lead: ◇K

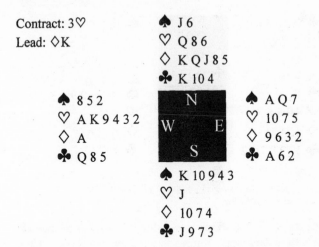

```
                    ♠ J 6
                    ♡ Q 8 6
                    ◇ K Q J 8 5
                    ♣ K 10 4
  ♠ 8 5 2              N           ♠ A Q 7
  ♡ A K 9 4 3 2                    ♡ 10 7 5
  ◇ A          W           E       ◇ 9 6 3 2
  ♣ Q 8 5              S           ♣ A 6 2
                    ♠ K 10 9 4 3
                    ♡ J
                    ◇ 10 7 4
                    ♣ J 9 7 3
```

You have lost a spade and will lose a heart. There is another spade to lose and so you need to avoid two club losers. One option is to play South for the ♣K, but how likely is that? North overcalled at the two-level vulnerable opposite a passed partner. Would North bid 2◇ with ♡Q-x-x, ◇K-Q-J-x-x and no more than one or two jacks in the black suits? Assuming North is a competent player, you should place the ♣K with North. You need to decide whether to play North for ♣K-x (play ♣A and duck a club) or for ♣K-x-x.

Ruff South's diamond exit and play a spade to the ace. South's early spade discard and North's ♠J looks like North began with two spades and so three clubs. Ruff a third diamond, cross to the ♣A and ruff dummy's last diamond. Then exit with a trump. North wins and can cash a diamond – you discard the spade loser – but then has to give you a club trick and so you make 3♡.

South can defeat 3♡ with a switch to a high club at trick 5. That is hardly an obvious move.

51. Dealer North : East-West vulnerable

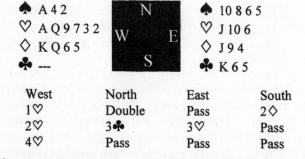

♠ A 10 8 6 2		♠ K J 5 3
♡ Q 7 3 2		♡ 6
◇ K 4		◇ Q 10 9 3
♣ Q 9		♣ K J 10 3

West	North	East	South
	Pass	Pass	2♡ (1)
Pass	2NT (2)	Double (3)	Pass
Pass	3♡	Pass	Pass
3♠	Pass	4♠	All pass

(1) 5-card weak two, 8-11 points   (2) Strong inquiry
(3) Takeout of hearts

North leads the ♡10: six – king – two. South switches to the ◇8:
four – ace – three and North returns the ◇2: nine – seven – king.
Plan your play.

Solution on page 86.

52. Dealer West: North-South vulnerable

♠ A 4 2		♠ 10 8 6 5
♡ A Q 9 7 3 2		♡ J 10 6
◇ K Q 6 5		◇ J 9 4
♣ ---		♣ K 6 5

West	North	East	South
1♡	Double	Pass	2◇
2♡	3♣	3♡	Pass
4♡	Pass	Pass	Pass

North leads the ♣A, which you ruff. Plan your play. Suppose
you cash the ♡A next and North discards a club. What next?

Solution on page 87.

53. Dealer East : North-South vulnerable

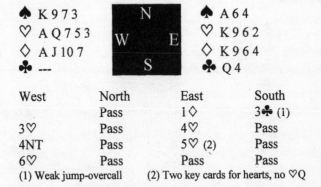

	♠ A 8 7			♠ K 9 6 5 4
	♡ K 4 3			♡ J 2
	◇ 2			◇ 8 7 4 3
	♣ A K Q 10 8 3			♣ 9 6

West	North	East	South
		Pass	Pass
1♣	1◇	1♡ (1)	Pass
1♠ (2)	2◇	2♠	Pass
4♠	Pass	Pass	Pass

(1) 4+ spades   (2) 3-4 spades

Transfer responses at the one-level are gaining popularity. North leads the ◇A: three – nine – two and continues with the ◇Q: four – jack – ♠7. Plan your play.
Solution on page 88.

54. Dealer North : Nil vulnerable

	♠ K 9 7 3			♠ A 6 4
	♡ A Q 7 5 3			♡ K 9 6 2
	◇ A J 10 7			◇ K 9 6 4
	♣ ---			♣ Q 4

West	North	East	South
	Pass	1◇	3♣ (1)
3♡	Pass	4♡	Pass
4NT	Pass	5♡ (2)	Pass
6♡	Pass	Pass	Pass

(1) Weak jump-overcall   (2) Two key cards for hearts, no ♡Q

North leads the ♣2, fourth-highest: four – king – ♡3. All follow when you play ♡A and a heart to the king. Plan your play.
Solution on page 89.

51. From a National Team Selection in 2010:

Contract: 4♠
Lead: ♡10

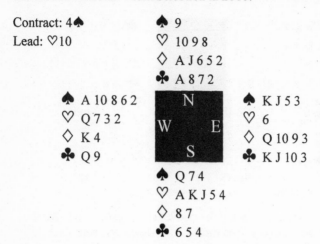

The problem revolves around avoiding a trump loser. In the Open Trials, seven pairs were in 4♠ and four succeeded. In the Women's division, seven pairs played 4♠ and all failed. At one table in the Open, South opened 1♡, West bid 1♠, North 2◇, East 4♠, all pass, but North thought for some time before passing. North was thinking of sacrificing. Had West taken that inference it would be reasonable to play North for shortage in spades. West thought North might have been contemplating a penalty double and so started with the ♠A and went down.

At another table, after the auction given, ♡10 to the king, ◇8 to the ace and the next diamond to West, how should West continue?

Australian expert, Paul Gosney, opted for a psychological move. He ruffed a heart in dummy and led the ◇Q. East pondered for a moment and then pitched a club. That was enough for declarer. Deducing that South had something to protect in trumps, West discarded a heart and continued with the ♠K and a spade to the ten. He ruffed his last heart, ruffed a diamond and cashed the ♠A. West conceded a trick to the ♣A, but he had ten tricks for +620.

52. From a National Team Selection in 2010:

Contract: 4♡
Lead: ♣A

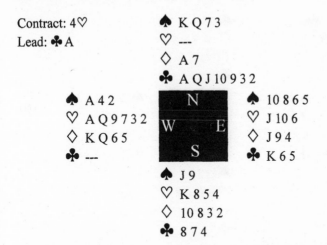

    ♠ K Q 7 3
    ♡ ---
    ◇ A 7
    ♣ A Q J 10 9 3 2

♠ A 4 2
♡ A Q 9 7 3 2
◇ K Q 6 5
♣ ---

♠ 10 8 6 5
♡ J 10 6
◇ J 9 4
♣ K 6 5

    ♠ J 9
    ♡ K 8 5 4
    ◇ 10 8 3 2
    ♣ 8 7 4

At one table West ruffed the ♣A lead and played ♡A and a heart to the ten and king. South switched to the ♠J. West took the ace, crossed to the ♡J and discarded a spade on the ♣K. The trouble was that declarer was now in dummy. After a diamond to the king and ace, he could not avoid losing a second diamond. One down.

A low heart lead at trick 2 works, but it does give up on ♡K being singleton. The bidding marks North with a strong hand. After the ♡A lead reveals the ♡K with South, it is highly likely that North has the ◇A. At trick 3 West should play a low diamond. If North ducks, the ◇J wins and West has a number of lines to succeed, all of which include ducking a diamond to drop the now bare ace.

At another table West was in 5♡ doubled and North led the ♣A. West won and played a low diamond (which also works in 4♡), low from North, jack. Then came ♡J, ♣K to discard a spade, club ruff and the ◇K, ace. West won the ♠K switch and played ◇Q, diamond ruff, and the ♡10, ducked. West was down to ♠4 and ♡A-Q. He exited with a spade and had 11 tricks.

53. From a National Open Teams in 2010:

Contract: 4♠
Lead: ◇A

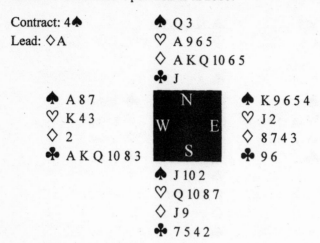

```
                    ♠ Q 3
                    ♡ A 9 6 5
                    ◇ A K Q 10 6 5
                    ♣ J
♠ A 8 7                              ♠ K 9 6 5 4
♡ K 4 3          N                   ♡ J 2
◇ 2            W   E                  ◇ 8 7 4 3
♣ A K Q 10 8 3    S                  ♣ 9 6
                    ♠ J 10 2
                    ♡ Q 10 8 7
                    ◇ J 9
                    ♣ 7 5 4 2
```

What should West do after ruffing the second diamond? You should aim to make use of the strong clubs. If trumps are 4-1, you are almost certain to fail. You hope that spades are 3-2 and the clubs 3-2 or 4-1 with the hand with three spades also having the length in clubs.

Your best hope is to play ♠A, ♠K and then start on the clubs. If you play a top club at trick 3, the fall of the ♣J should persuade you to draw a couple of rounds of trumps. As the cards lie, you collect three discards from dummy before South ruffs.

If South had started with three spades, five hearts, three clubs, then after ruffing the second diamond, West takes ♠A, ♠K and starts on the clubs, discarding two diamonds from dummy. South ruffs the fourth club, but has only hearts left. On a low heart from South, West would need to pick the position. On the bidding the ♡A figures to be with North.

On the actual deal East had the ♡Q and South the ♡J. That gave West other winning options.

54. From a Team Selection for national competition, 2010:

Contract: 6♡
Lead: ♣2

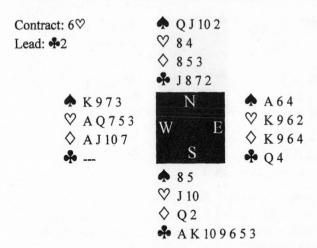

```
              ♠ Q J 10 2
              ♡ 8 4
              ♢ 8 5 3
              ♣ J 8 7 2
♠ K 9 7 3                    ♠ A 6 4
♡ A Q 7 5 3        N         ♡ K 9 6 2
♢ A J 10 7     W     E       ♢ K 9 6 4
♣ ---              S         ♣ Q 4
              ♠ 8 5
              ♡ J 10
              ♢ Q 2
              ♣ A K 10 9 6 5 3
```

At several tables South overcalled 2♣ and West frequently made twelve tricks by finessing South for the ♢Q. Given the two-level overcall, the ♢Q was very likely to be with South.

At the table where South overcalled 3♣, West reached 6♡ and North led the ♣2. West ruffed South's ♣K and drew trumps with ♡A, ♡K. After ♣Q, ace, ruffed, West played ♠A, ♠K and a third spade. This guaranteed the contract if spades were 3-3. Whoever took the third spade would have to lead a diamond or give West a ruff-and-discard. When North won and played the fourth spade, West ruffed and, as North had more diamonds than South, West finessed North for the ♢Q. One down.

The ♣2 opening lead marks South with at least seven clubs. After ruffing the club and ♡A, ♡K, ruff dummy's second club and cash ♠A, ♠K. When South follows to two spades, South cannot have more than two diamonds. Play the ♢A and run the ♢J. If North has the ♢Q, you are home. If South has it, South has to play a club and the ruff-and-discard eliminates dummy's spade loser.

55. Dealer East : North-South vulnerable

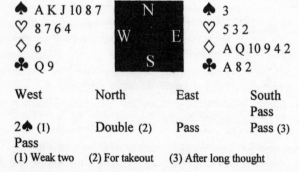

	♠ A K 10 6 5		♠ 9 7 3 2
	♥ A 5 2		♥ J 10 4
	◇ 7		◇ A 8
	♣ A 8 7 4		♣ K 6 5 2

West	North	East	South
		Pass	Pass
1♠	Pass	3♣ (1)	Pass
4♠	Pass	Pass	Pass

(1) 4+ spades, 6-9 points

North leads the ♣Q. Do you win this in dummy or in hand or do you duck? When you start on the trumps, South follows once and discards a diamond on the ♠K. Plan your play.

Solution on page 92.

56. Dealer South : North-South vulnerable

	♠ A K J 10 8 7		♠ 3
	♥ 8 7 6 4		♥ 5 3 2
	◇ 6		◇ A Q 10 9 4 2
	♣ Q 9		♣ A 8 2

West	North	East	South
			Pass
2♠ (1)	Double (2)	Pass	Pass (3)
Pass			

(1) Weak two   (2) For takeout   (3) After long thought

North leads the ♥A, ♥K, ♥J. South follows with ♥10, ♥Q, ♣6 (no club interest). North shifts to the ◇3. Plan your play.

Solution on page 93.

57. Dealer West : North-South vulnerable

	♠ 4		♠ K 9 7 5 2
	♡ A Q 9 8 6		♡ K 10 4
	◇ A J 2		◇ 8
	♣ A 7 3 2		♣ K Q 10 8

West	North	East	South
1♡	Pass	1♠	Pass
2♣	Pass	2◇ (1)	Pass
2♡	Pass	3♡	Pass
4NT	Pass	5♣ (2)	Pass
6♡	Pass	Pass	Pass

(1) Fourth-suit forcing   (2) One key card for hearts

North leads the ◇4: eight – queen – ace. Plan your play.
Solution on page 94.

58. Dealer North : Both vulnerable

	♠ 6		♠ A Q 10 9 7 2
	♡ A 10 7 5 4		♡ K J 2
	◇ K J		◇ 9
	♣ K Q 9 5 4		♣ A 7 3

West has reached 6♡ with no bidding by North-South.
North leads the ◇A and continues with the ◇4. You
discard a spade from dummy and capture South's ◇8.
You play a low heart, queen, king, followed by the ♡J,
♡A and ♡10, on which North discards three diamonds.
Plan your play.
Solution on page 95.

55. From a National Senior Team Selection in 2010:

Contract: 4♠
Lead: ♣Q

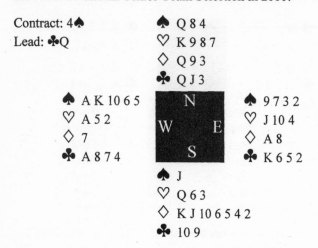

```
              ♠ Q 8 4
              ♡ K 9 8 7
              ◊ Q 9 3
              ♣ Q J 3
♠ A K 10 6 5        N        ♠ 9 7 3 2
♡ A 5 2       W         E    ♡ J 10 4
◊ 7                          ◊ A 8
♣ A 8 7 4          S         ♣ K 6 5 2
              ♠ J
              ♡ Q 6 3
              ◊ K J 10 6 5 4 2
              ♣ 10 9
```

At any other but unfavourable vulnerability, South might have opened 3◊. Some would do so anyway.

West should play low in dummy on the ♣Q lead. Your club spot cards are very powerful. By winning in hand with the ace, you can ensure you lose only one club trick if North has led from Q-J-10-3 or Q-J-9-3. As the clubs were 3-2 this precaution was not needed.

After the ♣A captures the ♣9, you play ♠A, ♠K. Once you find out that you have a spade loser and a club loser, you must try to lose only one heart trick. The best chance is to play for split honours. Play the ♣4: three – five – ten. If South exits with a low heart, you duck in hand. North wins, cashes the ♠Q and exits with a diamond. Take the ◊A and run the ♡J, playing South for the ♡Q.

After winning with the ♣10 South is more likely to exit with a diamond. Take the ◊A, ruff the ◊7, cash the ♣K and exit with a trump to North's ♠Q. A ruff-and-discard solves your problem. If North leads a low heart, play the jack, queen, ace and then lead a heart towards dummy, playing the ten if North follows low.

56. From the final of a National Pairs, 2010:

Contract: 2♠ doubled
Lead: ♡ A

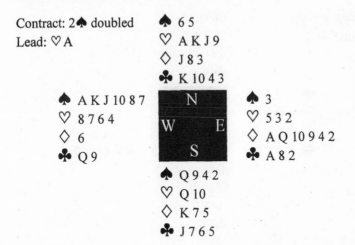

```
                ♠ 6 5
                ♡ A K J 9
                ◇ J 8 3
                ♣ K 10 4 3
♠ A K J 10 8 7              ♠ 3
♡ 8 7 6 4       N          ♡ 5 3 2
◇ 6          W     E       ◇ A Q 10 9 4 2
♣ Q 9           S          ♣ A 8 2
                ♠ Q 9 4 2
                ♡ Q 10
                ◇ K 7 5
                ♣ J 7 6 5
```

South's decision to pass North's takeout double for penalties is questionable with so few trumps and such poor ones. North began with three top hearts and should have played the fourth heart. That would have ensured one down, but opponents do err.

After North switched to the ◇3 at trick 4, how should West play? Even without South's discouraging club signal, West can place the ♣K with North. Without it, North would switch to a club, not a diamond. If the ♣K is with North, then ◇K is surely with South. Otherwise where is South's penalty pass?

You should play the ◇10 or ◇9 from dummy. South wins with the ◇K and switches to the ♣5. You try the ♣Q, but North covers and you take the ♣A. You discard a heart on the ◇A and a club on the ◇Q. The ♠3 to the seven, eight, ten or jack works as the cards lie. As you can reasonably expect South to have five spades for the penalty pass, it is sensible to play the ♠3 and insert the ♠7 or ♠8 when South follows low.

57. From the 2010 USA Open Team Trials:

Contract: 6♡   ♠ Q 8
Lead: ◇4   ♡ J 5 3
                                ◇ 9 6 5 4 3
                                ♣ 9 6 4

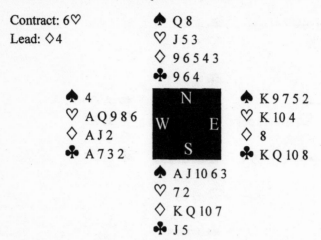

♠ 4   ♠ K 9 7 5 2
♡ A Q 9 8 6   ♡ K 10 4
◇ A J 2   ◇ 8
♣ A 7 3 2   ♣ K Q 10 8

                                ♠ A J 10 6 3
                                ♡ 7 2
                                ◇ K Q 10 7
                                ♣ J 5

West captured South's ◇Q and played the ♠4: eight – king – ace.
South returned a spade and West ruffed. Since the defenders knew
the spade position, the ♠Q was not necessarily a forced card.
South ruffed a diamond and ruffed a spade with the ♡9. North
over-ruffed with the ♡J and West was one down.

That was unlucky, to be sure, but there was no great urgency to
play a spade at once. West could easily have adopted the line at
the other table where the contract was 4♡ and where West made
12 tricks. Take the ◇A, ruff a diamond and play low spade from
dummy. Then you comfortably ruff the other diamond, cash the
♡K and return to hand to draw trumps. You use the ♣A and a
spade ruff as your entries. That would be +11 Imps instead of –11.

As the cards lie, it would also work to ruff a diamond at trick 2,
come to hand with the ♣A, ruff your remaining diamond and exit
from dummy with the ♠K. This line is not as attractive, since you
might suffer a trump promotion if South has the ♠A and North
began with ♡J-x-x and only three diamonds.

58. From the final round in the 2010 European Open Teams:

Contract: 6♡
Lead: ◊A

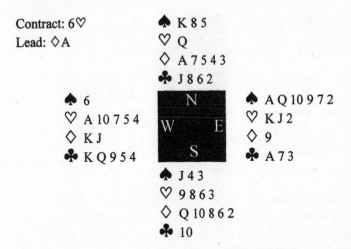

```
              ♠ K 8 5
              ♡ Q
              ◊ A 7 5 4 3
              ♣ J 8 6 2
  ♠ 6                          ♠ A Q 10 9 7 2
  ♡ A 10 7 5 4      N          ♡ K J 2
  ◊ K J          W     E       ◊ 9
  ♣ K Q 9 5 4       S          ♣ A 7 3
              ♠ J 4 3
              ♡ 9 8 6 3
              ◊ Q 10 8 6 2
              ♣ 10
```

In each of the four matches between eight leading teams, one side played in 6♡ and the other played game in hearts. The slam is not attractive, as you are off an ace and the trump queen. At some tables West bid 4NT and East replied 5◊, three key cards. Unable to locate the ♡Q cheaply, West bid 6♡. You can find out how to solve this problem in the new *Improve Your Slam Bidding*.

One North led the ♣6: three – ten – king. West played a low heart, queen, king, and a diamond to the jack and North's ace. North played another club and South ruffed. One down and –13 Imps.

The other three Norths led ◊A and another diamond. West played a low heart, queen, king, followed by the ♡J and two more top hearts, drawing trumps. Two declarers tried ♣K and a club to the ace, receiving the bad news. After taking the ♣Q they finessed the ♠Q. That won, but they still had a loser and were one off. The German declarer played ♣K, ♣Q, leaving the ♣A in dummy. If the clubs behaved he was home. When they did not, he finessed the ♠Q, cashed ♠A and ruffed a spade for +1430 and +13 Imps.

59. Dealer West : Both vulnerable

♠ A K Q 8 7   ♠ J 9 5
♥ A 9 4 2   ♥ 7
♦ A J 9   ♦ 6 2
♣ 4   ♣ A K Q J 10 7 3

West	North	East	South
1♠	Pass	2♣	Pass
2♥	Pass	3♠	Pass
4NT	Pass	5♦	Pass
5NT	Pass	7♠	All pass

The 5NT bid promised than no key cards were missing and so
East bid 7♠ based on the solid clubs. North leads the ♥8.
Plan your play. How would you play if the contract is 6♠?
Solution on page 98.

60. Dealer East : North-South vulnerable

♠ 7   ♠ K J 5 4
♥ K J 10 8 2   ♥ A 7 6 5
♦ A 9 6 2   ♦ K 8 4
♣ A 7 5   ♣ 9 8

West	North	East	South
		Pass	1♠
2♥	Pass	2♠ (1)	Pass
4♥	Pass	Pass	Pass

(1) Strong heart raise, maximum pass

North leads the ♠10. Plan your play.
Solution on page 99.

61. Dealer South : East-West vulnerable

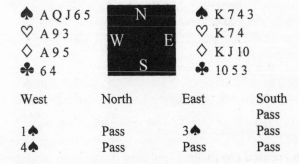

♠ A Q 3		♠ J 7 2
♡ A 8 7 5 3		♡ Q 10 2
◊ A 10 6		◊ 7 3
♣ Q 5		♣ K J 8 7 2

West	North	East	South
			Pass
1♡	2♡ (1)	3♡	Pass
4♡	Pass	Pass	Pass

(1) 5+ spades, 5+ minor

North leads the ♠10. Which card do you play from dummy? As there is no benefit to being in dummy at trick 1, you play low, ♠K from South. You win and play the ♡A: king – two – four. Plan your play.

Solution on page 100.

62. Dealer South : Both vulnerable

♠ A Q J 6 5		♠ K 7 4 3
♡ A 9 3		♡ K 7 4
◊ A 9 5		◊ K J 10
♣ 6 4		♣ 10 5 3

West	North	East	South
			Pass
1♠	Pass	3♠	Pass
4♠	Pass	Pass	Pass

North leads the ♠10. Trumps split 3-1. Plan your play.
Solution on page 101.

59. From a National Open Teams, 2010:

Contract: 7♠
Lead: ♡8

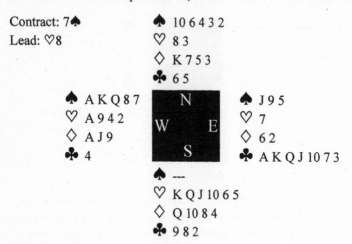

```
                  ♠ 10 6 4 3 2
                  ♡ 8 3
                  ◇ K 7 5 3
                  ♣ 6 5
  ♠ A K Q 8 7          N          ♠ J 9 5
  ♡ A 9 4 2         W     E       ♡ 7
  ◇ A J 9              S          ◇ 6 2
  ♣ 4                              ♣ A K Q J 10 7 3
                  ♠ ---
                  ♡ K Q J 10 6 5
                  ◇ Q 10 8 4
                  ♣ 9 8 2
```

You can count 5 spades, 7 clubs and 2 aces. As usual, when your contract looks simple, consider bad breaks. What could go wrong? The only threat is a 5-0 spade split, but you can deal with that easily enough.

Take the ♡A and cash the ♠A. South shows out and so you finesse the ♠9, cash the ♠J, cross to the ◇A, draw the trumps and claim. If North had shown out you can unblock the ♠9 under the ♠A, cross to the ♠J and finesse against South on the third spade, then draw trumps and claim. The play should be exactly the same in 6♠.

What trap must you avoid? Do not start trumps with a low spade to the jack. Do not ruff a heart at trick 2. That is pointless.

Datum: East-West 900. Ten pairs played in 4♠ and six in 3NT. Three played in 6♣ and one was in 7♣. There were 13 in 6♠ and nine failed. They probably received a club lead. One made 6NT doubled. Three played 7♠ and three were in 7NT, all succeeding. 7NT is certainly the best contract.

60. From the 2010 Rosenblum (World Open Teams):

Contract: 4♡
Lead: ♠10

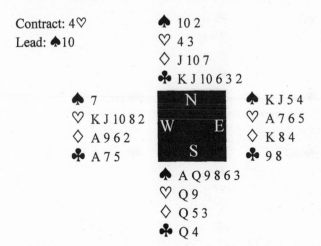

```
                    ♠ 10 2
                    ♡ 4 3
                    ◇ J 10 7
                    ♣ K J 10 6 3 2
        ♠ 7            N          ♠ K J 5 4
        ♡ K J 10 8 2              ♡ A 7 6 5
        ◇ A 9 6 2   W      E      ◇ K 8 4
        ♣ A 7 5        S          ♣ 9 8
                    ♠ A Q 9 8 6 3
                    ♡ Q 9
                    ◇ Q 5 3
                    ♣ Q 4
```

There were 102 pairs in 4♡ and 69 declarers were successful.
One world champion West went off this way. He covered the
♠10 lead with the jack, won by South with the queen. Reluctant
to continue spades, South switched to the ♣4. West took that and
decided to play North for the ♡Q. After ♡K, the ♡J was run to
South's queen. The defenders cashed a club and West still had to
lose a diamond for one down.

The declarer at the other table found a better move. He ducked the
opening lead. When the ♠10 held, North played a second spade.
West ruffed and played ♡A, ♡K. Then came three rounds of
diamonds. When they were 3-3, West could discard a club from
dummy and so he made an overtrick and +11 Imps.

The actual spade position was highly likely on the bidding and the
opening lead. Playing the ♠J meant that a club switch was highly
likely. Now success would depend on no trump loser. Ducking the
♠10 allows you to test hearts *and* diamonds if North continues
spades. If you play ♡A, ♡K and the queen has not dropped, you
still make if diamonds are 3-3.

61. From a National Open Teams, 2011:

Contract: 4♡
Lead: ♠10

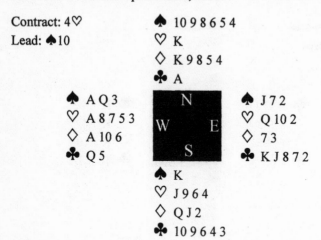

♠ 10 9 8 6 5 4
♡ K
◇ K 9 8 5 4
♣ A

♠ A Q 3
♡ A 8 7 5 3
◇ A 10 6
♣ Q 5

♠ J 7 2
♡ Q 10 2
◇ 7 3
♣ K J 8 7 2

♠ K
♡ J 9 6 4
◇ Q J 2
♣ 10 9 6 4 3

From trick 1 you can deduce that North has six spades. With ♠K-x, South would play low, after dummy played low, in case North's ♠10 lead was from ♠Q-10-9-x-x. Hence the ♠K is singleton and so North began with six spades.

When you play the ♡A and North produces the ♡K, that is also clearly a singleton. With South having ♡J-9-6-4 you have two heart losers and you are bound to lose one club. That means you cannot afford a diamond loser.

You need to discard your diamond losers on two club winners in dummy. North's 5-card minor is unknown, but there is no chance if North began with five clubs. You have to play for North to be 6-1-5-1 with the singleton ♣A. That is not likely, but there is no other hope. Australian expert Bill Jacobs played the ♣5 and the miracle layout existed. North won and played the ♠9, jack, ruffed. South returned the ◇Q. West took the ace, cashed the ♣Q, crossed to the ♡Q and pitched two diamonds on dummy's top clubs. That was +420 and +10 Imps as 4♡ went one down at the other table. Datum: East-West 70.

62. From a National Youth Teams, 2011:

Contract: 4♠
Lead: ♠10

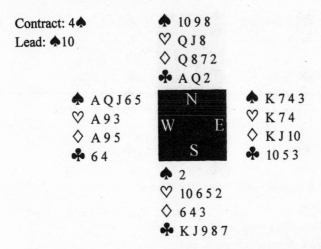

```
                    ♠ 10 9 8
                    ♡ Q J 8
                    ◇ Q 8 7 2
                    ♣ A Q 2
     ♠ A Q J 6 5         N         ♠ K 7 4 3
     ♡ A 9 3                       ♡ K 7 4
     ◇ A 9 5        W       E      ◇ K J 10
     ♣ 6 4                         ♣ 10 5 3
                        S
                    ♠ 2
                    ♡ 10 6 5 2
                    ◇ 6 4 3
                    ♣ K J 9 8 7
```

A 5-3-3-2 pattern opposite a 4-3-3-3 often makes the same number of tricks in no-trumps as in the 5-3 or 5-4 trump fit. If that number of tricks is nine, then you want to be in 3NT. At teams, if West opens a strong 1NT, East should raise to 3NT. Although this can be beaten on a club lead, will North find that start? If the bidding begins 1NT : Pass : 2♣ : Double, you must play 4♠ and not 3NT.

If North leads a heart against 4♠, the defence can collect a heart and two clubs. Declarer now has to locate the ◇Q.

After the ♠10 lead, trying to guess the diamond finesse is a 50% chance, but declarer has a 100% play. Draw the missing trumps and then play a club. Win the heart return with the ace and lead another club. Take the next heart with dummy's king and ruff dummy's last club. Now exit with your third heart. The defence is helpless. A club or a heart would give West a ruff-and-discard and a diamond would solve the guess there.

63. Dealer West : North-South vulnerable

♠ J 10 9 5 4		♠ A Q 7	
♡ A Q 6 3		♡ 4 2	
◇ K 9		◇ A Q 6 4	
♣ A K		♣ J 9 8 3	

West	North	East	South
1♠	Pass	2♣	Pass
2♡	Pass	3♠	Pass
4NT	Pass	5♠ (1)	Pass
6♠	Pass	Pass	Pass

(1) Two key cards for spades plus the ♠Q

North leads the ◇7: four – ten – king. You play the ♠J: three –
seven – six. Plan your play.

Solution on page 104.

64. Dealer North : Nil vulnerable

♠ A 3 2		♠ Q J 9 6	
♡ J		♡ A 9 3	
◇ A Q 8 4 2		◇ 7 6	
♣ A J 7 2		♣ K 9 4 3	

West	North	East	South
	Pass	Pass	Pass
1◇	Pass	1♠	Pass
2♣	Pass	3♣	Pass
3♠	Pass	4♣	Pass
5♣	Pass	Pass	Pass

North leads the ♣5: three – eight – jack. Plan your play.

Solution on page 105.

65. Dealer West : Both vulnerable

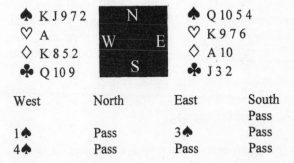

♠ Q J 10 9 8 4 2		♠ A 3
♡ 3		♡ K J 8 7
◇ K Q 4		◇ J 8
♣ A 4		♣ K J 10 8 3

West	North	East	South
1♠	Pass	2♣	Pass
2♠	Pass	3♡	Pass
3♠	Pass	4♠	All pass

North leads the ◇9: eight – two – king. North-South play reverse signals, low-encouraging. Plan your play.
Solution on page 106.

66. Dealer South : Nil vulnerable

♠ K J 9 7 2		♠ Q 10 5 4
♡ A		♡ K 9 7 6
◇ K 8 5 2		◇ A 10
♣ Q 10 9		♣ J 3 2

West	North	East	South
			Pass
1♠	Pass	3♠	Pass
4♠	Pass	Pass	Pass

North leads the ♡J. Plan your play.
Solution on page 107.

63. From the 2011 NEC Cup:

Contract: 6♠
Lead: ◇7

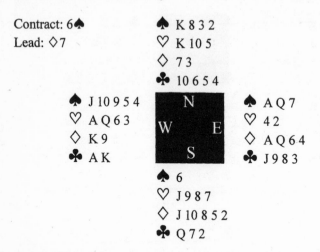

```
                 ♠ K 8 3 2
                 ♡ K 10 5
                 ◇ 7 3
                 ♣ 10 6 5 4
 ♠ J 10 9 5 4        N        ♠ A Q 7
 ♡ A Q 6 3      W        E    ♡ 4 2
 ◇ K 9               S        ◇ A Q 6 4
 ♣ A K                        ♣ J 9 8 3
                 ♠ 6
                 ♡ J 9 8 7
                 ◇ J 10 8 5 2
                 ♣ Q 7 2
```

You would fail if you relied on the heart finesse. There is no urgency to take that finesse or to go for a heart ruff. You can discard one heart on the third diamond and you might find some luck in the clubs.

After the ♠J won trick 2, the winning play produced at the table by Yoshiyuki Nakamura of Japan was: ♣A; ♣K; spade to the queen; low club, queen, ruffed; spade to the ace; ♣J, discarding a heart; ◇A; ◇Q, discarding another heart and North, with only the ♠K and hearts left, was stymied. In practice North discarded a heart, too, but West ruffed the fourth diamond, exited with a spade and claimed his slam.

Two other declarers made 6♠. Both received a club lead. There were 22 declarers who went one down in 6♠, eleven on the ◇7 lead, seven on a low club lead and four on the ♠2 lead.

64. From the 2010 Rosenblum (World Open Teams):

Contract: 5♣
Lead: ♣5

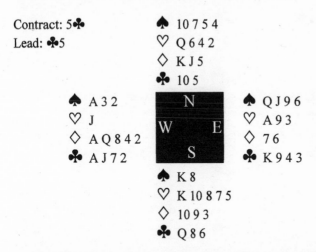

```
                    ♠ 10 7 5 4
                    ♡ Q 6 4 2
                    ◇ K J 5
                    ♣ 10 5
    ♠ A 3 2            N            ♠ Q J 9 6
    ♡ J                             ♡ A 9 3
    ◇ A Q 8 4 2     W     E         ◇ 7 6
    ♣ A J 7 2          S            ♣ K 9 4 3
                    ♠ K 8
                    ♡ K 10 8 7 5
                    ◇ 10 9 3
                    ♣ Q 8 6
```

After winning trick 1 with the ♣J, West played the ♡J to the ace and ruffed a heart. A low spade went to the queen and king and South returned the ♠8, won in dummy. Declarer ruffed dummy's third heart and West cashed the ♣A. When West played the ♠A, South was able to ruff. The diamond finesse lost later and so the contract was one down.

There is a useful play principle here. With a choice between ruffing losers and establishing a long suit, it is usually better to set up the long suit. Play a heart to the ace at trick 2 and take the diamond finesse. Although the diamond finesse loses, you can set up the diamonds and eleven tricks are easy.

That is what happened in another match after South opened 1♡ in third seat (why?) and North led the ♡2. Declarer took the ♡A and finessed the ◇Q. He ruffed the heart return, played the ◇A and ruffed a diamond. Next came the ♠Q, king, ace, followed by the ♣K, ♣A and diamond winners. The defence could take no more than the ◇K and the ♣Q.

65. From a National Open Teams, 2011:

Contract: 4♠
Lead: ◇9

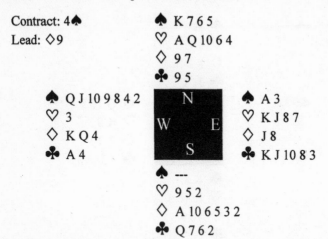

        ♠ K 7 6 5
        ♡ A Q 10 6 4
        ◇ 9 7
        ♣ 9 5

♠ Q J 10 9 8 4 2   ♠ A 3
♡ 3   ♡ K J 8 7
◇ K Q 4   ◇ J 8
♣ A 4   ♣ K J 10 8 3

        ♠ ---
        ♡ 9 5 2
        ◇ A 10 6 5 3 2
        ♣ Q 7 6 2

At one table, West opened 4♠. That might be all right in third or
fourth seat, but the hand is too strong for a pre-empt first-in-hand.
All passed and North led the ◇9: eight – ace – four. South
returned a diamond and there was no realistic way for North-
South to score more than one spade, one heart and one diamond.

At the other table, West opened 1♠ and also ended in 4♠ after
the given auction. North led the ◇9 and, judging that West was
more likely to have three diamonds than four, South played low.
West won and ran the ♠Q, followed by a spade to the ace. He
continued with the ♡K. North took the ace and returned the ◇7.
South won and gave North the diamond ruff and that was one
down and +12 Imps.

After winning the first diamond, West should realize the danger
of a diamond ruff and simply play a diamond straight back. You
should plan to ruff the third diamond and that will allow you to
make 4♠ in comfort.

66. From the 2009 European Open Teams:

Contract: 4♠
Lead: ♡J

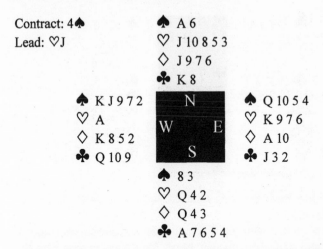

```
                    ♠ A 6
                    ♡ J 10 8 5 3
                    ◇ J 9 7 6
                    ♣ K 8
♠ K J 9 7 2                        ♠ Q 10 5 4
♡ A              N                 ♡ K 9 7 6
◇ K 8 5 2     W     E              ◇ A 10
♣ Q 10 9         S                 ♣ J 3 2
                    ♠ 8 3
                    ♡ Q 4 2
                    ◇ Q 4 3
                    ♣ A 7 6 5 4
```

With 30 tables in play, the common contract was 4♠ by West, generally after 1♠ : 3♠, 4♠, all pass. Most declarers failed, some after North led the ♣K and received a club ruff and others after winning the heart lead and playing a trump. North lost no time in taking the ♠A and switching to ♣K and another club. South won and played a third club for North to ruff.

Two successful declarers were Eric Rodwell (USA) and Ton Bakkeren (Netherlands). They received the ♡J lead and foresaw the possible danger of a club ruff. After winning with the ♡A they both took precautionary measures by crossing to the ◇A and cashing the ♡K to discard a club. Only then did they lead a trump and the danger had been averted.

67. Dealer West : East-West vulnerable

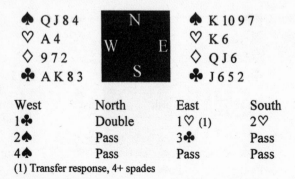

	♠ Q J 8 4		♠ K 10 9 7
	♡ A 4		♡ K 6
	◇ 9 7 2		◇ Q J 6
	♣ A K 8 3		♣ J 6 5 2

West	North	East	South
1♣	Double	1♡ (1)	2♡
2♠	Pass	3♣	Pass
4♠	Pass	Pass	Pass

(1) Transfer response, 4+ spades

After North leads the ♡5, what do you know about the North-South hands?

You win trick 1 with the ♡K and lead a spade to your queen. North wins and plays another heart. You draw trumps with the ♠K, ♠J, North having started with ♠A-x-x. You lead a diamond to the queen and South's king. South shifts to the ♣7. Your play?

Solution on page 110.

68. Dealer West : Both vulnerable

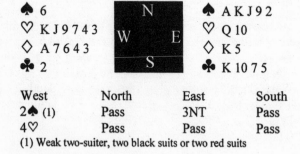

	♠ 6		♠ A K J 9 2
	♡ K J 9 7 4 3		♡ Q 10
	◇ A 7 6 4 3		◇ K 5
	♣ 2		♣ K 10 7 5

West	North	East	South
2♠ (1)	Pass	3NT	Pass
4♡	Pass	Pass	Pass

(1) Weak two-suiter, two black suits or two red suits

North leads the ♠4. Plan your play.

Solution on page 111.

69. Dealer South : North-South vulnerable

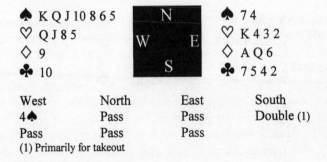

	♠ 9 2		♠ 7 5
	♡ K J 7 3		♡ A
	◇ A K 10 7 4		◇ 9 8 6 3 2
	♣ J 9		♣ A Q 8 4 2

West	North	East	South
			Pass
1◇	2◇ (1)	4♣ (2)	4♠
Pass	Pass	5◇	Double
Pass	Pass	Pass	

(1) Two-suiter, hearts and spades   (2) Fit-showing jump

North leads the ♠Q. South takes the ♠K, ♠A and shifts to the ♣3: nine – king – ace. Plan your play.

Solution on page 112.

70. Dealer West : North-South vulnerable

	♠ K Q J 10 8 6 5		♠ 7 4
	♡ Q J 8 5		♡ K 4 3 2
	◇ 9		◇ A Q 6
	♣ 10		♣ 7 5 4 2

West	North	East	South
4♠	Pass	Pass	Double (1)
Pass	Pass	Pass	

(1) Primarily for takeout

North leads the ♡6. Plan your play.

Solution on page 113.

67. From a National Senior Teams, 2010:

Contract: 4♠
Lead: ♡5

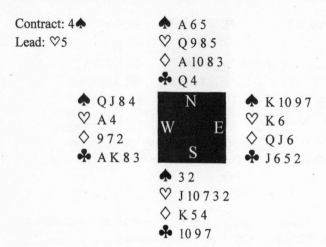

```
                    ♠ A 6 5
                    ♡ Q 9 8 5
                    ◇ A 10 8 3
                    ♣ Q 4

♠ Q J 8 4                         ♠ K 10 9 7
♡ A 4                             ♡ K 6
◇ 9 7 2                           ◇ Q J 6
♣ A K 8 3                         ♣ J 6 5 2

                    ♠ 3 2
                    ♡ J 10 7 3 2
                    ◇ K 5 4
                    ♣ 10 9 7
```

At the table West won the heart lead in dummy and led a trump to the queen and ace. North continued with a heart. Declarer played the ♠K and a spade to the jack, followed by a diamond to the queen and king. South shifted to the ♣7. West ducked. North won and the contract was one down.

Given the bidding, West should be able to deduce the location of the ♣Q at trick 1. East-West have 24 HCP and so North-South have 16. The ♡5 opening lead implies North's hearts are not headed by the Q-J. It would be normal to lead the top heart otherwise. With A-K in diamonds, North would probably have led a top diamond. That marks South with at least the ♡J and ◇K. North should have all the remaining high cards to justify the takeout double (which itself is no thing of beauty). Therefore play ♣A, ♣K later in the play. Your play is rewarded when the ♣Q drops on the second club.

68. From a match between Australia and Singapore, 2011:

Contract: 4♡
Lead: ♠4

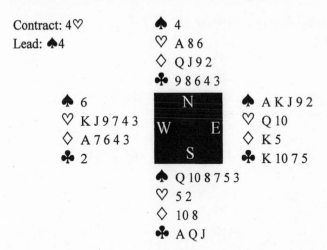

♠ 4
♡ A 8 6
◇ Q J 9 2
♣ 9 8 6 4 3

♠ 6
♡ K J 9 7 4 3
◇ A 7 6 4 3
♣ 2

♠ A K J 9 2
♡ Q 10
◇ K 5
♣ K 10 7 5

♠ Q 10 8 7 5 3
♡ 5 2
◇ 10 8
♣ A Q J

West should have passed 3NT, which is very easy to make. At the other table East-West had an artificial auction to 4♡ by West.

At both tables North led the ♠4, taken by the ace. Both declarers muffed the play when they continued with the ♠K, pitching the ♣2. Both Souths gave suit-preference signals for clubs. The Singapore North ruffed and continued with the ♡A and a second heart. Declarer later lost two diamonds for one down.

At the other table the Australian North failed to take advantage of declarer's slip. He ruffed the ♠K and should have played two rounds of trumps. When he switched to a club, West ruffed, played ◇K, ◇A, diamond ruff, club ruff, diamond ruff and had ten tricks for +620 and +12 Imps.

Both declarers had a blind spot. After taking the ♠A, West should play ◇K, ◇A, diamond ruff, and then discard the ♣2 on the ♠K. West can afford to lose a diamond, a heart and a club.

69. From the 2011 Rosenblum, Round of 32:

Contract: 5◊ doubled
Lead: ♠Q

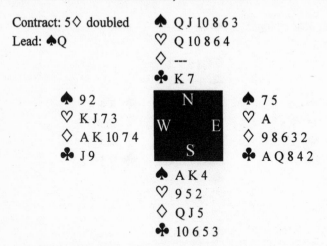

♠ Q J 10 8 6 3
♡ Q 10 8 6 4
◊ ---
♣ K 7

♠ 9 2
♡ K J 7 3
◊ A K 10 7 4
♣ J 9

♠ 7 5
♡ A
◊ 9 8 6 3 2
♣ A Q 8 4 2

♠ A K 4
♡ 9 5 2
◊ Q J 5
♣ 10 6 5 3

At both tables West was in 5◊ after North showed both majors and South bid spades. At one table 5◊ was passed out. North led the ♠Q. South overtook and cashed another spade. He then switched to the ◊5. West rose with the ◊A and went one down.

At the other table South doubled 5◊ after the auction given and the play began similarly with the ♠Q lead, taken by the ♠K and the ♠A cashed. At this table South switched to the ♣3, king, ace. Matt Mullamphy played a diamond and inserted the ◊10 when South followed with the ◊5. When that held, he drew trumps and had eleven tricks for +550 and +12 Imps.

There are two reasons to choose this play in diamonds. Where is South's double with nothing more than two top spades and only one or two diamonds? You might also expect a diamond void with North, who has bid 2◊, vulnerable against not, opposite a passed partner, and has very modest high card strength in the majors.

70. From a Butler Open Trials, 2010:

Contract: 4♠ doubled
Lead: ♡6

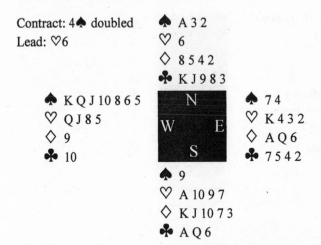

        ♠ A 3 2
        ♡ 6
        ♢ 8 5 4 2
        ♣ K J 9 8 3

♠ K Q J 10 8 6 5   ♠ 7 4
♡ Q J 8 5   ♡ K 4 3 2
♢ 9   ♢ A Q 6
♣ 10   ♣ 7 5 4 2

        ♠ 9
        ♡ A 10 9 7
        ♢ K J 10 7 3
        ♣ A Q 6

To pre-empt with a side 4-card major is not recommended, but
sometimes it can work to your advantage. Given South's takeout
double, the ♡6 lead is almost certainly a singleton. You can see
what might easily happen: ♡A, heart ruff, club to the ace, heart
ruff, ♠A for two down, –300. That would still be a good result, as
North-South can make 5♣ or 6♢.

Hoping to avoid the heart ruff, West played low from dummy and
dropped the ♡J under South's ♡A. South picked West for a
singleton heart or ♡Q-J doubleton, and shifted to the ♣A. Now
West was one down at worst. When South continued with the ♣6,
West ruffed and led the ♠Q, winning. North won the next spade
and switched to a diamond. West rejected the diamond finesse. He
took the ♢A, ruffed a club and then played out the spades. With
one trump to go West had ♠5 ♡Q-8-5, East ♡K-4 ♢Q-6 and
South had ♡10-9-7 ♢K. When West played the ♠5 and discarded
the ♢6 from dummy South was finished.

71. Dealer South : Both vulnerable

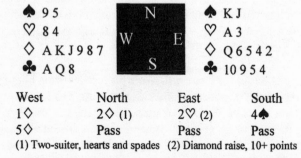

	♠ A 6 5 4		♠ K Q
	♡ K 9 8 6		♡ ---
	◇ J 4 3		◇ A K Q 8 7
	♣ 4 3		♣ A K J 10 7 2

West	North	East	South
			2♡ (1)
Pass	3♡ (2)	4NT (3)	Pass
5◇	Pass	5♡ (4)	Pass
5♠ (4)	Pass	7◇	All pass

(1) Weak two   (2) Pre-emptive raise   (3) Both minors
(4) Cue-bid, first-round control

North leads the ♡5. Plan your play.
   Solution on page 116.

72. Dealer West : North-South vulnerable

	♠ 9 5		♠ K J
	♡ 8 4		♡ A 3
	◇ A K J 9 8 7		◇ Q 6 5 4 2
	♣ A Q 8		♣ 10 9 5 4

West	North	East	South
1◇	2◇ (1)	2♡ (2)	4♠
5◇	Pass	Pass	Pass

(1) Two-suiter, hearts and spades   (2) Diamond raise, 10+ points

North leads the ♠A and switches to the ♡J, taken by the ace. You cash the ◇A and all follow. You cross to the ♠K and play the ♡3. South wins with the ♡Q and leads the ♣6. What is North's shape? Which club do you play from hand?

   Solution on page 117.

73. Dealer East : Nil vulnerable

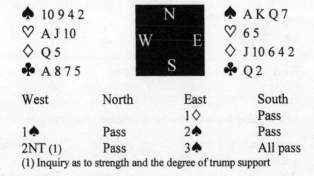

	♠ ---		♠ Q 3
	♡ Q 8 4 3		♡ A J 6 2
	◇ A K Q J 9 4		◇ 10 3
	♣ A 9 6		♣ Q 7 5 3 2

West	North	East	South
		Pass	Pass
1♣ (1)	4♠	Double (2)	Pass
5◇	Pass	Pass	Pass
(1) Artificial, 15+ points		(2) For takeout	

North leads the ♠A. You ruff and play ◇A, ◇K. North discards a spade on the second diamond. Plan your play.
Solution on page 118.

74. Dealer East : North-South vulnerable

♠ 10 9 4 2		♠ A K Q 7
♡ A J 10		♡ 6 5
◇ Q 5		◇ J 10 6 4 2
♣ A 8 7 5		♣ Q 2

West	North	East	South
		1◇	Pass
1♠	Pass	2♠	Pass
2NT (1)	Pass	3♠	All pass
(1) Inquiry as to strength and the degree of trump support			

North leads the ♠8. Plan your play. Trumps are 3-2.
Solution on page 119.

71. From a Butler Open Trials, 2011:

Contract: 7◊
Lead: ♡5

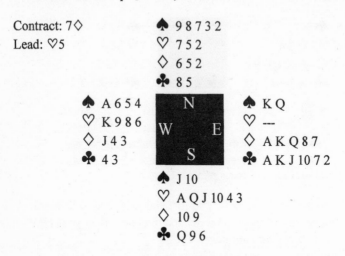

♠ 9 8 7 3 2
♡ 7 5 2
◊ 6 5 2
♣ 8 5

♠ A 6 5 4
♡ K 9 8 6
◊ J 4 3
♣ 4 3

♠ K Q
♡ ---
◊ A K Q 8 7
♣ A K J 10 7 2

♠ J 10
♡ A Q J 10 4 3
◊ 10 9
♣ Q 9 6

Have you noticed North's values for the raise to 3♡? Don't try this at home, folks. If East doubled and West passed, the defence can collect eight tricks easily for +1100. On the other hand, that is still cheaper than East-West making 6◊ or 7◊. As the datum was East-West 970, only about half the field bid even the small slam in diamonds.

Note that 7◊ is not hard to make as the cards lie. Ruff the heart lead, cash ◊A and ◊K. When trumps break, play ♣A, ♣K, ruff a club with the ◊J, cross to dummy with a spade, draw the last trump and claim. If South shows out on the second diamond, play a trump to the jack and take the club finesse. Assuming it wins, draw the last trump, overtake a spade with the ace and repeat the club finesse. Given the weak 2♡ opening, the chances are good that the ♣Q is onside.

72. From a Butler Open Trials, 2010:

Contract: 5◇
Lead: ♠A

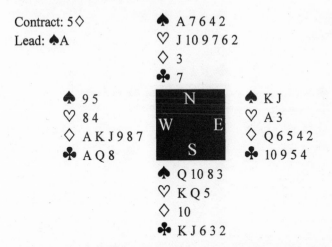

♠ A 7 6 4 2
♡ J 10 9 7 6 2
◇ 3
♣ 7

♠ 9 5
♡ 8 4
◇ A K J 9 8 7
♣ A Q 8

♠ K J
♡ A 3
◇ Q 6 5 4 2
♣ 10 9 5 4

♠ Q 10 8 3
♡ K Q 5
◇ 10
♣ K J 6 3 2

West should be able to deduce North's shape. With 4-4 in the majors, South might have jumped to 4♡ since it appears that South's hearts are stronger than the spades. A more likely action by South with 4-4 majors would be to bid 4◇, asking North to choose the longer or stronger major.

South's 4♠ bid therefore implies that South has more spades than hearts. In that case North will have at least six hearts and might have a 5-6-1-1 pattern.

When South returns a club, playing the ace will work if North has king-bare (a 1-in-6 chance), playing the queen will work if North has jack-bare (a 1-in-6 chance) and playing a low club will work whenever North has any low singleton (a 4-in-6 chance). On that basis West should play the ♣8 on the ♣6. That worked on the actual layout and also succeeds if North has a 5-7-1-0 pattern.

73. From the 2010 USA Open Team Trials:

Contract: 5♦
Lead: ♠A

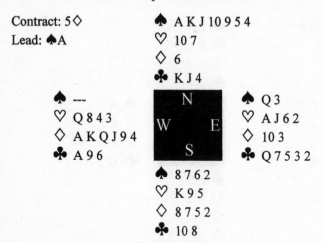

♠ A K J 10 9 5 4
♡ 10 7
♦ 6
♣ K J 4

♠ ---
♡ Q 8 4 3
♦ A K Q J 9 4
♣ A 9 6

♠ Q 3
♡ A J 6 2
♦ 10 3
♣ Q 7 5 3 2

♠ 8 7 6 2
♡ K 9 5
♦ 8 7 5 2
♣ 10 8

At one table West opened 1♦ and North bid 4♠, Pass, Pass, back to West, who doubled for takeout. East passed the double and led the ♦10. North ruffed the second diamond, drew trumps and played a heart to the king, followed by a club to the king. A club ruff later was enough for ten tricks and +590.

At the other table, after the auction given, West was in 5♦. He ruffed the spade lead and played ♦A, ♦K. He abandoned trumps and played a heart to the jack. That lost and back came a spade, ruffed. West could not afford to draw trumps now and so played the ♣A and another club. North won and gave South a club ruff. One down.

West must hold the club losers to one or play North for ♡K-x. West should draw all the trumps, discarding a spade and a heart, and test the clubs before hearts. After ♣A and another club, West rises with dummy's ♣Q if North plays the ♣J. A third club sets up two winners in dummy. Now two of West's losers vanish on dummy's clubs and the heart finesse is not needed. West makes six diamonds, four clubs and one heart.

74. From a National Open Teams, 2011:

Contract: 3♠
Lead: ♠8

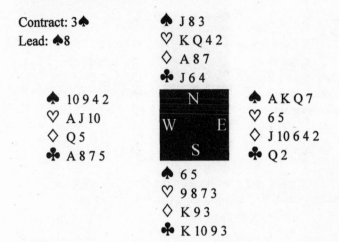

```
                    ♠ J 8 3
                    ♡ K Q 4 2
                    ◇ A 8 7
                    ♣ J 6 4
  ♠ 10 9 4 2              N          ♠ A K Q 7
  ♡ A J 10                           ♡ 6 5
  ◇ Q 5          W         E         ◇ J 10 6 4 2
  ♣ A 8 7 5              S           ♣ Q 2
                    ♠ 6 5
                    ♡ 9 8 7 3
                    ◇ K 9 3
                    ♣ K 10 9 3
```

West's 2NT was an inquiry and 3♠ showed four spades, but a
minimum opening. Declarer won the spade lead with the ♠Q and
continued with the ♠K, ♠A. The plan was simple: play the ◇Q,
win any return and play another top diamond, set up the diamonds
and lose one heart, one club and two diamonds.

West's plan was flawed and North exacted punishment. Declarer
led a low diamond to the queen. Had North taken this, 3♠ would
succeed, but North ducked. West lacked the entries to set up the
diamonds and went one down.

The solution was to start on the side suit before drawing all the
trumps. Play ♠Q, ♠K, then a diamond to the queen. Now a duck
by North will be of no avail and 3♠ will make.

75. Dealer West : Both vulnerable

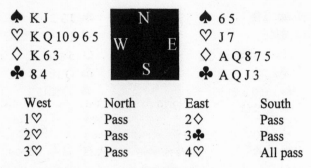

♠ K J
♡ K Q 10 9 6 5
◇ K 6 3
♣ 8 4

♠ 6 5
♡ J 7
◇ A Q 8 7 5
♣ A Q J 3

West	North	East	South
1♡	Pass	2◇	Pass
2♡	Pass	3♣	Pass
3♡	Pass	4♡	All pass

North leads the ◇J and you win with the ◇K. You play the ♡9: two – seven – ace. South switches to the ♠4. Your play?

Solution on page 123.

76. Dealer North : Nil vulnerable

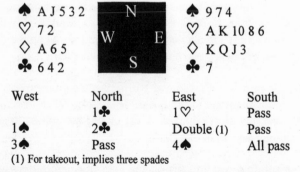

♠ A J 5 3 2
♡ 7 2
◇ A 6 5
♣ 6 4 2

♠ 9 7 4
♡ A K 10 8 6
◇ K Q J 3
♣ 7

West	North	East	South
	1♣	1♡	Pass
1♠	2♣	Double (1)	Pass
3♠	Pass	4♠	All pass

(1) For takeout, implies three spades

North leads the ♣K – seven – eight (reverse count) – two. North switches to the ◇10, taken by the king. You play the ♠4: eight – two – six and South continues with the ♠10, ace, queen. Plan your play. How would you play if South returns a club after winning with the ♠8?

Solution on page 124.

77. Dealer East : Nil vulnerable

♠ A K 10 7	N	♠ J 3 2
♡ K		♡ 10 9
♢ A K Q 10 6 2	W E	♢ 5 4 3
♣ J 3	S	♣ Q 10 7 4 2

West	North	East	South
		Pass	Pass
1♢	1♡	Pass	4♡
4♠	Pass	Pass	Pass

North leads the ♣8 to South's ace and South returns the ♣6 to North's ♣K. North cashes the ♡A and then reverts to the ♣9: queen – five and you discard a diamond. Plan your play.

Solution on page 125.

78. Dealer East : North-South vulnerable

♠ K Q 7 6 3	N	♠ A 10 2
♡ 7 3 2		♡ A K J 5
♢ A J 6	W E	♢ 10 5 4 3
♣ K 6	S	♣ 10 7

West	North	East	South
		1♣	Pass
1♠	Pass	1NT	Pass
2♢ (1)	Pass	2♡	Pass
2♠	Pass	3♠	Pass
4♠	Pass	Pass	Pass

(1) New minor forcing

North leads the ♢7: three – queen – ace. You play ♠K, ♠Q and a spade to the ace. North follows and South discards a club. You continue with the ♢4: eight – jack – two. How do you proceed?

Solution on page 126.

79. Dealer South : East-West vulnerable

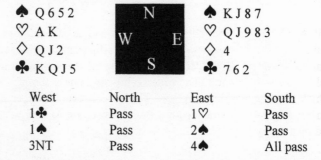

♠ 5 3 2		♠ A Q 9 7 4
♡ A Q 10		♡ 7
◇ Q 10 2		◇ A 5
♣ 10 8 7 2		♣ A Q 9 4 3

West	North	East	South
			1◇
Pass	1♡	2◇ (1)	Double (2)
2♠	Pass	3♠	Pass
4♣	Pass	Pass	Pass

(1) At least 5-5 in spades and clubs   (2) Exactly three hearts

North leads the ◇6. Plan your play.
    Solution on page 127.

80. Dealer West : East-West vulnerable

♠ Q 6 5 2		♠ K J 8 7
♡ A K		♡ Q J 9 8 3
◇ Q J 2		◇ 4
♣ K Q J 5		♣ 7 6 2

West	North	East	South
1♣	Pass	1♡	Pass
1♠	Pass	2♠	Pass
3NT	Pass	4♠	All pass

North leads the ◇6: four – ace – two. South switches to the ♣A: five – three – two, followed by the ♣4: king – nine – six. Plan your play.
    Solution on page 128.

75. Board 4, Round 17, 2011 World Team Championships:

Contract: 4♡
Lead: ◇J

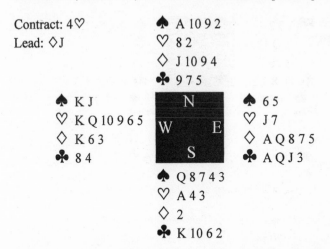

```
                        ♠ A 10 9 2
                        ♡ 8 2
                        ◇ J 10 9 4
                        ♣ 9 7 5
    ♠ K J                              ♠ 6 5
    ♡ K Q 10 9 6 5                     ♡ J 7
    ◇ K 6 3                            ◇ A Q 8 7 5
    ♣ 8 4                              ♣ A Q J 3
                        ♠ Q 8 7 4 3
                        ♡ A 4 3
                        ◇ 2
                        ♣ K 10 6 2
```

After West won trick 1 and led the ♡9 to South's ace, South switched to the ♠4 and declarer had a 50-50 guess. It was a straight guess. There were no clues in the bidding to indicate which opponent was more likely to have the ♠A.

Still, there can be other clues, such as the choice of lead. You can make life easier for yourself when such situations arise. Assume that the opening leader declined to lead the critical suit because he held the ace in that suit. Therefore you would put in the ♠J here, which was the winning decision. This clue is even stronger here, since the unbid suit was spades, but North chose to lead the suit bid by dummy.

Even if East-West had an artificial, relay auction to 4♡, you can still work on the premise that North's failure to lead a spade makes it a little bit more likely that North has the ace. Another thought on the actual hand is the idea of split aces. As South has turned up with the ♡A, the ♠A figures to be with North.

76. From the quarter-finals, 2011 World Team Championships:

Contract: 4♠
Lead: ♣K

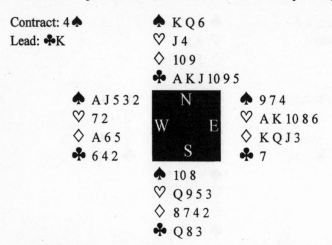

```
                    ♠ K Q 6
                    ♡ J 4
                    ◊ 10 9
                    ♣ A K J 10 9 5
♠ A J 5 3 2                          ♠ 9 7 4
♡ 7 2                                ♡ A K 10 8 6
◊ A 6 5                              ◊ K Q J 3
♣ 6 4 2                              ♣ 7
                    ♠ 10 8
                    ♡ Q 9 5 3
                    ◊ 8 7 4 2
                    ♣ Q 8 3
```

After you win the diamond switch with the king and play a spade, ducking South's ♠8, you are in good shape if South returns the ♠10 and North follows on your ♠A. You can ruff one club loser and discard the other on the fourth diamond. You simply have to do it in the right order. Play the diamonds first. North can ruff the third diamond, but you can then claim. If you ruff the club loser first and then play diamonds, North ruffs the third round and cashes a club. One down.

If South returns a club after winning with the ♠8, you ruff in dummy. You cannot afford to cross to the ◊A and play the ♠A. North can ruff the third diamond and cash a club.

After ruffing the club, come to the ◊A and ruff your other club loser. Then cash the ♡A, ♡K, followed by diamonds. North can ruff the third diamond and play a club, but you win and ♠A draws the missing trumps. After ruffing the third club it would be an error to play diamonds without cashing the ♡A, ♡K first. North would ruff the third diamond and play a heart. Dummy wins and you cannot avoid North scoring another trump trick.